Financial Responsibilities
OF GOVERNING BOARDS

BY WILLIAM S. REED

Financial Responsibilities of Governing Boards *is made possible by generous grants from Commonfund and KPMG, LLP.*

**Association of Governing Boards
of Universities and Colleges**
One Dupont Circle • Suite 400
Washington, D.C. 20036
www.agb.org

NACUBO
2501 M Street NW, Suite 400
Washington, D.C. 20037
www.nacubo.org

Contents

Foreword

Change is a constant in higher education, and no one is spared the resulting impact, including the nation's university and college trustees. But what is new at the start of the millennium is a rise in the stakes. Competition from for-profit education providers, a technology revolution that threatens to bust budgets, and an increasingly cost-conscious public have combined to ratchet up the need for effective trustees and governing boards.

Although financial responsibilities are by no means the sole duties of conscientious trustees, we believe that sound stewardship of an institution's endowment, budget and planning processes, personnel policies, and physical plant is central to the contribution trustees make to an institution's well-being.

This completely redone edition of *Financial Responsibilities of Governing Boards* encompasses a strategically important slice of what trustees need to know. The goal of inculcating financial savvy within governing boards is shared with equal enthusiasm by the two organizations that collaborated in its publication—the Association of Governing Boards of Universities and Colleges and the National Association of College and University Business Officers.

To update the material for an era characterized by a widespread sense that higher education has sailed into uncharted waters, we decided the task called for an individual with exceptionally broad experience and wisdom. Author William S. Reed not only brings to the project 30 years of experience in finance-related positions in higher education, he writes with a disarming style that weaves in a healthy dose of alternative viewpoints. Both of us claim him as a good friend and colleague, and we thank him for his superb labor of love in writing this book. We also thank our colleagues at Commonfund and KPMG for contributing to the publication costs of this volume.

The result, we think, is an authoritative and thought-provoking primer on the financial responsibilities of trustees and on complex emerging trends and issues bearing on the responsibilities of governing boards. It should serve as an invaluable arrow in the quivers of all leaders in higher education.

Richard T. Ingram
President
Association of Governing Boards
of Universities and Colleges

James E. Morley, Jr.
President
National Association of College
and University Business Officers

February 2001, Washington, D.C.

About William S. Reed

Will Reed's career spans 40 years in academic institutions and nonprofit organizations. His background is broad and covers all of the major financial and administrative areas. He has been a chief financial officer, a chief development officer, and a chief human resources officer. In addition, he has served as an administrative officer of a foundation and as a government contracts officer. He received his undergraduate degree from Kenyon College and his masters of public administration from the Maxwell School of Public Affairs at Syracuse University.

Will began his career in 1961 with the U.S Atomic Energy Commission, for which he negotiated contracts with major research universities. In 1967, he moved to the Ford Foundation as an administrative officer in India and later in New York. His next move was to be the director of personnel for Princeton University from 1973-77. He then moved to Kenyon College, where he served as vice president of development from 1977-80, and then to Williams College, where he was vice president for administration and treasurer, and secretary of the board, until 1990. He was the vice president of finance and administration at Wellesley College until 2000. He currently serves as Wellesley's vice president of the college.

Will also chairs two education-related boards. First is the Boston Consortium for Higher Education, which was created in 1995 to reduce administrative costs through collaboration. Member institutions are Babson, Bentley, Boston College, Boston University, Harvard, Northeastern, MIT, Olin, Tufts, Wellesley, and Wheaton.

Second is the School, College, University, Underwriters, Ltd. (SCUUL), an organization that exemplifies how colleges and universities can collaborate to solve common problems. Some 50 academic institutions collectively invested $40 million to start this for-profit company. Today, it is the nation's largest provider of liability insurance to colleges and universities. In addition, he is the vice president of the board of directors of the Williamstown Theatre Festival.

Will is a frequent contributor to professional publications and has conducted numerous seminars on financial issues for AGB and NACUBO.

Acknowledgments

This book was made possible by generous grants from Commonfund and KPMG, LLP and through the efforts of AGB and NACUBO. While I am the sole author and take responsibility for the content, this book truly is a collaborative effort. I would like to thank and acknowledge the contributions of many colleagues:

The directors of SCUUL and United Educators helped frame the contents of the book. They include Janice Abraham, president and chief executive officer, United Educators; Ralph Beaudoin, vice president and treasurer, Catholic University of America; Roger Blunt, former vice chair, University of Maryland Board of Regents; Chuck Bunting, chancellor, Vermont State College; Carol Campbell, vice president and treasurer, Texas Christian University; Ruth Constantine, vice president, Smith College; Andrew Evans, vice president and treasurer, Oberlin College; James Hatcher, president, Educational and Institutional Insurance Administrators, Inc.; Mary Jo Maydew, treasurer, Mt. Holyoke College; Dale McGirr, vice president of finance, University of Cincinnati; David Lascell, partner, Hallenbeck, Lascell, Norris and Zorn and trustee, Grove City College; James Maniford, vice president of business affairs and treasurer, Scripps College; Ed Shannahan, president and headmaster, Choate Rosemary Hall; Burt Sonenstein, president and chief executive officer, SCUUL; and Liz Williams, treasurer, Southern Methodist University.

My colleagues at Wellesley College also have helped with this book. I am particularly grateful to President Diana Walsh, Vice President for Planning Pat Byrne, Budget Director Linda Murphy Church, Chief Investment Officer Catherine Feddersen, and my administrative assistant, Janet Sullivan. Two Wellesley trustees gave timely advice—Walter Cabot, also treasurer of Wellesley, and Victoria Herget, board chair.

In 1998, Wellesley gave me the wonderful gift of a semester sabbatical, which I devoted to researching this book. I also was given an appointment as a visiting practitioner at the Harvard Graduate School of Education. While at Harvard, I had the privilege of working with Richard Chait, a noted authority on trusteeship and governing boards, and with James Honan, who teaches a popular graduate course on managing financial resources in nonprofit organizations. By osmosis in that stimulating environment, I learned a great deal about the theory and practice of academic trusteeship.

My former colleagues at Williams College helped shape my views on what it means to be a fiduciary of an academic institution. In particular, I would like to acknowledge the work and influence of John Chandler, former president of Williams College; Michael S. McPherson, president of Macalester College; Morton Owen Schapiro, president of Williams; and Gordon C. Winston, an economist at Williams and a principal in the Williams Project on the Economics of Higher Education.

Joel W. Meyerson, president of the Forum for the Future of Higher Education at Yale University, has been a close friend and colleague over the years. Through him, I have met some of the most thoughtful and insightful thinkers on the future of higher education.

Over the course of my career, I have been privileged to work closely with Cambridge Associates and Commonfund. Much of the material for the chapter on endowments is derived from my conversations with them and from their published materials.

Special thanks are due to the scores of trustees who participated in the sessions on the board's financial responsibilities at AGB's national conferences and to my copresenters, Brenda Norman Albright and Robert Turner. Many of the ideas presented in the book were developed at these seminars.

Several people at AGB also worked hard to shape and improve this book. AGB Board Chair A. Marshall Acuff, Jr.

helped shape the publication in its early stages. Senior Editor Deborah Bongiorno worked tirelessly to encourage me to meet deadlines. Everything I submitted, she improved. To Deborah, heartfelt thanks for her patience and editing skills. President Tom Ingram, Executive Vice President Richard D. Legon, and Senior Editor Susan Shoulet made useful suggestions in the final stages, and Vice President for Publications Daniel J. Levin shepherded it through the editing and publishing process.

At NACUBO, President Jay Morley and Senior Vice President Larry Goldstein also provided substantive reviews, as did Jim McGill of Johns Hopkins University and Elaine Watson of DePaul University.

Finally, I wish to express my admiration and respect for the 50,000 thoughtful, talented, resourceful, and hardworking citizens who serve as higher education trustees. Their service and dedication has helped create an educational system that truly is the envy of the world.

William S. Reed
Wellesley, Mass.
February 2001

Introduction

The purpose of this book is to help trustees understand the issues that surround the exercise of their financial responsibilities. Trustees must deal with a complex blend of competing values, evolving information, and challenging analyses while taking into account the academic culture of their institutions and the context of higher education. Colleges and universities are complicated organizations that can be difficult to understand, especially for corporate executives who are accustomed to making speedy—sometimes unilateral—decisions and who may be held accountable only for an organization's bottom-line performance.

Working with dedicated boards and their members can be an exhilarating experience. Boards provide a forum, a conscience, an institutional memory, and a critical support system for senior management. Some trustees truly are extraordinary. They share a high level of commitment to their institution's mission, an ability to focus on strategic issues, a caring toughness, and an appreciation of what it means to be a fiduci-ary. This book is intended to help trustees as well as chief financial offi-cers—especially those in the independent sector but also those in public higher education, where the basic principles espoused here should prevail. Its goal is to describe how trustees exercise their fiduciary responsibilities and to help veterans and newcomers alike better understand the range of financial issues most colleges and universities confront.

The Association of Governing Boards of Universities and Colleges (AGB) and the National Association of College and University Business Officers (NACUBO) first published *Financial Responsibilities of Governing Boards* in 1979. The book was revised in 1985. This new edition is intended to be a companion to AGB's *Understanding Financial Statements*, by John H. McCarthy and Robert M. Turner with Sandra L. Johnson, which was published in 1998.

When AGB President Tom Ingram and NACUBO President Jay Morley first asked me to update and rewrite this book, I declined. My hesitation stemmed from the fact that I was engaged in the daily battles of being a chief financial officer of a liberal arts college. I also reckoned that the first two editions had been bestsellers, and I knew it would be hard to add much to the content and insights that had proved to be so helpful to trustees over so many years.

The previous editions were written by distinguished panels of business officers. Tom and Jay convinced me that an updated version, written by a single author who had a broad range of experience in academic institutions and with governing boards, would be a useful addition to the literature on trusteeship. The deal we struck was that I would write a book that would be generic in content to ensure its relevance most particularly to trustees and finance officers of independent colleges but also to their peers in public higher education.

I also wanted to write a book that had a little edge to stimulate thought and discussion within boards. And so I began what turned out to be a two-year process of creating a new version of *Financial Responsibilities of Governing Boards*.

So much has changed since the book originally was published. Chief among those changes is the public's attitude about the value, accessibility, and affordability of higher education. Boards today face new challenges that have significant financial overtones; a book addressing them would be lacking if it did not discuss those financial responsibilities in the greater context of external challenges. These challenges include the following:

• **Heightened competition**. Higher education operates in a demanding and highly competitive marketplace. Competition exists on multiple levels: Colleges and universities compete for students, faculty, research grants, state funds, benefactors, and prestige.

Students, as tuition-paying customers, have heightened expectations for a variety of services they expect to receive. Additionally, information technology has added a new dimension to the competitive forces surrounding higher education. Every college and university, regardless of its mission, must have up-to-date computing facilities and services. Yet no one can safely predict the effect of new technology on teaching and learning, nor can anyone determine how distance learning will influence student choice. Admissions officers and others already have added virtual universities to the list of competitors they monitor.

The challenge for boards: to ensure the institution is positioned to remain competitive in a demanding, shifting, and uncertain environment.

• **Cost containment**. The issue of cost containment is high on the agenda of all institutions, regardless of financial condition. Further, all institutions feel pressure to slow the rate of growth in tuition and fees and to improve productivity and efficiency—all while increasing services.

At the core of the cost-containment issue is access and affordability. How can colleges and universities deliver the highest quality education for the least amount of tuition? Most institutions have reduced staff, reengineered administrative processes, borrowed management techniques from the for-profit world, and conducted countless cost-cutting studies. But the effect of all this activity on the quality of education is still not known.

We do know, however, that few

institutions have made fundamental, transformational cost reductions. Rather, most have tried to make administrative functions more efficient. The next round of cost reductions will have to reach beyond administrative areas into classrooms. Here's why: Higher education is labor intensive. An institution's most valuable—and expensive—asset is its faculty and staff. Compensation represents from 50 percent to 60 percent of the total cost of most operating budgets and can be as high as 80 percent in some community colleges. Hence, achieving permanent reductions in the cost base of the operating budget inevitably requires a reduction in the number of people on the payroll.

The challenge for boards: to ensure that reducing the payroll will not diminish the institution's intellectual capital.

• **Change**. Absent a crisis, change comes slowly and incrementally to most academic institutions. Many have tradition-bound cultures and governance structures that are devoted to maintaining the status quo. Nevertheless, the world is changing all around higher education, and the pressures to change are enormous.

To bring about effective change, institutional leaders must keep one foot grounded in the past and the other poised to step toward the future. In the coming years, the most successful institutions will be led by strategists who know how to maintain flexibility and continuity, and who can envision and prepare for the future.

The challenge for boards: to create and support an institutional climate that encourages administrators to anticipate change rather than merely to react to it.

• **Public support**. Public confidence in higher education is wavering. Opinion makers in the media have learned that higher education's "bad news" sells newspapers and attracts viewers. The public is worried that the cost of higher education is out of control, that the quality of higher education is slipping, that professors and others in academia do not work hard enough, and that colleges and universities are not being held accountable for this state of affairs. Higher education no longer possesses the special status it once enjoyed.

Consequently, academic leaders find themselves on the defensive as they try to answer increasingly aggressive, often vitriolic, criticism. Growing public concern about higher education's accountability has serious long-term implications for funding and support. Tuition-paying parents and students, as well as tax-paying citizens, want to know whether they are getting their money's worth. This is not a simple question to answer.

The challenge for boards: to respond to issues, crises, and opportunities forthrightly, with conviction, and with good data.

Obviously, no trustee can be fully conversant in all of these areas. But by gaining a better understanding of the work of finance-related committees, trustees can more fully appreciate the issues and tradeoffs of financial decision making.

This book is written with a strong

point of view—a clear set of beliefs about the responsibilities trustees assume for financial oversight of their institution. The following principles constitute the book's foundation:

1. To be capable of effectively exercising their fiduciary responsibilities, trustees should have a basic understanding of the financial condition of their institution. Responsibility for strategic financial decisions should not be delegated to the administration. Trustees should rely on senior administrators to make specific recommendations, but they should not shy from asking good questions and suggesting different paths to needed solutions. Unquestioned acceptance of all staff recommendations is an abdication of duty and can be disastrous for the institution, bad for the board and administration, and unfair to students and parents. It is careless policymaking. Trustees need to know their institution and the marketplace in which it competes if they are to understand the trade-offs inherent in most financial decisions.

2. Trustees should approach their financial responsibilities with common sense. One doesn't have to be a certified public accountant, financial analyst, or corporate executive to be an effective fiduciary. The most effective way for a board to exercise its financial responsibilities is through constant, careful monitoring of institutional goals, policies, and strategic indicators.

3. The financial condition of an institution should not be the exclusive knowledge of a handful of trustees and senior administrators. Full disclosure

leads to broad-based support when leaders address financial issues. Colleges and universities are inherently complex; thus, it is the responsibility of the president and chief financial officer to present financial information and frame issues with a clarity that enables all trustees to make informed decisions. Indeed, the faculty also needs to understand the institution's financial health.

4. The board and senior administrators must work as partners. The relationship should be built on understanding, trust, mutual respect, and an appreciation of one another's responsibilities for institutional governance. The working relationships between trustee committee chairs and their administrative counterparts are especially significant because their responsibilities intersect at the critical junction between policy and operations. These individuals should consult and agree on committee agendas, topics to research, and on the level of financial detail necessary to keep the entire board properly informed.

It is readily apparent that a primary responsibility of governing boards and individual trustees is to set a superb example with regard to their collective and individual philanthropy. Participation in fund-raising, especially within independent colleges and universities, is essential, and even within the public sector this expectation is being slowly but surely accepted. Moreover, some fiduciary issues are attached to the subject of fund-raising, including how to count gifts and pledges, accounting standards for comprehensive campaigns, and the importance of capacity-building. But this book does not include a chapter on this important subject because one chapter cannot possibly do justice to the topic and because the topic of fund-raising is beyond the purview of this book. Much literature on the topic already exists, including several titles AGB has published.

Finally, because many college and university trustees also serve on corporate boards, a word about some of the distinctions between the types of boards may be helpful. Trustees who serve on corporate boards quickly discover that the questions one asks as a trustee differ from the questions one might ask as a director of a for-profit organization. Why? Even though both kinds of boards have fiduciary responsibilities, the expectations are quite different. The primary difference is a simple fact: No one "owns" a college or university. Higher education institutions have stakeholders, not shareholders. These include current and prospective students, faculty, employees, alumni, donors and benefactors, accrediting agencies, government and community leaders, the surrounding community, sports fans, and citizens everywhere who benefit from the research that is conducted and the talents and skills of the institution's graduates. These stakeholders have a legitimate interest in the well-being of the institution, but they are not owners.

In contrast, corporate shareholders are owners. As such, they expect a profit —a return on their investment. College and universities do not have profits to distribute.

If there is an operating surplus, the institution will reinvest it; it will not be paid out as a dividend.

William G. Bowen, the president of the Andrew W. Mellon Foundation and former president of Princeton University, summed up the difference in the book, *Inside the Boardroom* (John Wiley & Sons, Inc. 1994): "For-profit boards concentrate on developing and carrying out broad strategies for enhancing shareholder values. Nonprofit boards are much more committed to the particular mission of their own organization." To further emphasize this point, Bowen quotes the former chairman of Goldman Sachs, a trustee of Haverford College: "A for-profit board has an obligation to get out of a bad business, while a nonprofit board may have an obligation to stay in, if it is to be true to its mission."

Trustees of colleges and universities hold their institutions in trust. And while there are no "owners" of a college or university, trustees have a responsibility to *think like owners*. Directors of corporations are responsible to the shareholders, and their primary job is to increase shareholder value. Trustees carry a heavier burden. Holding an institution in trust requires the interests of all stakeholders to be considered, even those who are yet to be born. That is why being a trustee is such an honor and requires commitment and dedication.

CHAPTER 1

Understanding Fiduciary Responsibilities

By most accounts, a governing board's most important duties are to appoint and support a president and to monitor his or her performance. The president is the board's agent for fulfilling the institution's mission and is directly responsible and accountable to the board. It is through the president that the board's policies are carried out. But the nuances of responsible trusteeship go beyond these propositions, and the exercise of fiduciary accountability is complex. Still, the job description of a governing board has remained consistent through the years:

- set and clarify the institution's mission and purposes,
- appoint the president,
- support the president,
- monitor the president's performance,
- assess board performance,
- insist on strategic planning,

- ensure good management,
- review educational and public-service programs,
- participate in fund-raising by giving and persuading others to do so,
- preserve institutional independence,
- relate campus to community and community to campus, and
- serve occasionally as a court of appeals.

An Institution's Culture. A stint on a college or university governing board can be full of surprises. Routine decisions may be misunderstood, and the board may be criticized for being insensitive to the institution's culture. Rarely does a major decision satisfy all constituents. Good communication is important in any organization, and especially so in an academic setting where the precise use of language is so critical. In fact, *how* a board communicates its decisions often is as important as *what* it decides to do.

To be effective, trustees should understand their institution's way of doing business. What cultural norms hold the institution together? What does the institution value most? Where does the real power reside? The answers to these questions will help trustees know what achievements are possible.

Because trustees are on campus for a limited amount of time, they sometimes have difficulty gaining more than a cursory sense of the institution, let alone understanding its unique culture. Though they naturally must guard against superficial analysis, trustees nonetheless can learn a great deal in a limited amount of time through disciplined observations and by being sensitive to nuance. Furthermore, opportunities such as board retreats, new-trustee orientation programs, and other board-development activities help reveal shared myths, values, traditions, and sacred cows.

To gain insight into an institution, trustees might do the following:

• Observe the lines of communication within the campus community. Are issues openly presented and debated? Are opposing views respected and considered? Organizations that foster a culture of direct and forthright communication tend to have high morale.

• Observe how well the senior staff functions as a team. It is difficult to have a well-functioning senior staff unless its members share a high level of trust.

• Monitor relationships between the faculty and the administration. Although some tension commonly exists between these two groups, it should not cause mistrust.

• Assess the level of trust among board members and between the board and senior management team. Is communication open and honest? Does debate focus on issues and policies rather than on politics and personalities? Is the staff adequately prepared? Is the board confident that the administration has explored all options thoroughly before asking the board to vote on an issue?

Trustees need to know their institutions well enough to understand which issues really matter. Ultimately, the board must have an accurate reading of the institution's culture if it is to perform its functions well.

An Institution's Values. Certain core values and beliefs are common to higher education. Among them are academic freedom; faculty control of the curriculum; collaboration with faculty on certain governance matters; emphasis on teaching, research, and service; and the unfettered exchange of ideas. When these core values (or others important to a particular sector of higher education) are threatened, turmoil usually is inevitable.

Boards must be particularly sensitive to an institution's core values, especially those held by faculty, and be prepared to explain and defend actions that would seem to contradict or challenge those values. Institutional values define standards of behavior, provide a context for priority setting, shape its image and reputation, and define its success. An institution's values can be expressed in many ways—through a student honor code, by creating and supporting a multicultural community, by adhering to participatory decision making, and by rewarding academic excellence and rigor, to name a few.

Trustees can discover their institution's values in many ways. Read annual reports, viewbooks, student publications, news releases, strategic plans, and similar documents. Pay careful attention to the values supported by institutional leaders in words and deeds—especially financial deeds. While on campus, observe what people actually do: how they treat each other, how they spend their time, what issues generate discussion, and what events or milestones are celebrated.

Culture, values, and governance are linked by the allocation of resources. The board is responsible for ensuring that institutional funds are allocated in accordance with institutional values. Without adequate resource support, important values reflect more myth than reality.

Governance. The diffused authority and responsibility that accompany academic trusteeship mystify many trustees. The faculty continues to have a predominant voice in academic affairs, including such matters as personnel decisions, curriculum development, and oversight. In other words, the faculty has primary responsibility for the main enterprise of the institution—teaching and learning. Although the governing board retains the ultimate legal responsibility for all institutional programs, it normally exercises that responsibility through the resource-allocation process and by

controlling the number of tenured positions. At the same time, however, trustees should not shy away from asking questions about the quality of the institution's programs. Ideally, board members should have a reasonably clear sense of which programs are particularly strong and which are not—and why.

Governance structures of most higher education institutions are quite similar. Differences lie in institutional size and complexity. Although a research university's governance structure differs in complexity from that of a liberal arts college, the two share many features: an independent governing board, a small group of senior executives who are considered "officers of the college," a faculty that oversees academic programs, and a tradition of collaboration on major decisions that affect the institution's condition and future strategic decisions. A college really has many leaders, and it is the job of the president to bring these leaders into alignment with his or her own goals and priorities and those of the board.

Stewardship of Institutional Assets. Colleges and universities hold many financial, physical, and human assets. Most campus leaders also regard their institution's reputation as an institutional asset. Being a fiduciary means holding an institution's assets in trust. It also means having adequate insurance to replace physical assets that are vulnerable to loss and to lower the institution's risk and exposure as much as possible.

Essential to oversight of asset preservation is reliable information. Trustees must be certain they receive accurate, current, relevant, and usable financial information. Boards must be confident that management has adequate controls in place to ensure accurate financial reporting and proper use of funds. Further, trustees must be confident that information distributed to the general public, public authorities, students, parents, donors, and granting agencies is truthful. The board's audit committee oversees financial reporting and works with an outside auditor to ensure the accuracy of reports. The audit committee and the full board must receive accurate, reliable, and timely data and information. If not, the first task is to do whatever it takes to get them.

Stewardship of Resources. This responsibility is carried out in various ways from one institution to the next, but at the heart of the matter is the need to ensure fidelity to the institution's mission and to secure the financial resources necessary to carry out its mission. In this regard, the board's financial responsibilities are inseparable from its overall responsibilities.

Almost nothing happens at a college or university without funding. How resources are spent determines how an institution fulfills its mission. The exercise of trusteeship is really about the stewardship of an institution's assets, which involves determining how funds are spent or preserved. As a fiduciary, each board member has a duty to ensure that funds are expended to support and

advance the institution's mission. This is the board member's public trust.

Stewardship and Prudence. College and university governing boards (including boards of foundations affiliated with public higher education institutions and systems) must exercise their stewardship with the care, skill, and diligence of a "prudent person." The definition of a "prudent act or decision" is open to interpretation, but there are a number of guidelines.

The Uniform Prudent Investor Act (UPIA), drafted in 1994 by the National Conference of Commissioners on Uniform State Laws, provides specific guidance. Consider this language from the prefatory note of the act:

[T]he act draws upon the revised standards for prudent trust investment promulgated by the American Law Institute in its *Restatement (Third) of Trusts: Prudent Investor Rule* (1992) and makes five fundamental alterations in the former criteria for prudent investing. They follow:

1. The standard of prudence is applied to any investment as part of the total portfolio, rather than to individual investments. In the trust, setting the term "portfolio" embraces all the trust's assets.

2. In all investing, the tradeoff between risk and return is identified as the fiduciary's central consideration.

3. All categoric restrictions on types of investments have been abrogated; the trustee can invest in any-

thing that plays an appropriate role in achieving the risk/return objectives of the trust and that meets the other requirements of prudent investing.

4. The long-familiar requirement that fiduciaries diversify their investments has been integrated into the definition of prudent investing.

5. The much-criticized former rule of trust law forbidding the trustee to delegate investment and management functions has been reversed. Delegation is now permitted, subject to safeguards.

The prefatory note further points out that "although the UPIA-1994 by its terms applies to trusts, not charitable corporations, the standards of the act can be expected to inform the investment responsibilities of directors and officers of charitable corporations. As the 1992 restatement declares, 'the duties of the members of the governing board of a charitable corporation are generally similar to the duties of the trustee of a charitable trust.' Absent contrary statute or other provision, the prudent investor rule applies to investment of funds held for charitable corporations."

Colleges and universities are charitable corporations and therefore subject to UPIA provisions. Boards should institute investment policies and procedures that comply with the act's provisions. In addition, the 1972 Uniform Management of Institutional Funds Act authorizes the boards of nonprofit institutions to delegate investment matters either to a committee of the board or to outside invest-

ment advisers, investment counsel, managers, banks, or trust companies. Various states emphasize different aspects of these acts in their adoption and implementation.

Trustees should understand the extent of their personal liability for decisions they make on behalf of their institution. In most states, volunteers are protected from civil liability by statute in certain circumstances if they act negligently in carrying out their duties, unless they acted knowingly or with gross negligence. Many states allow nonprofit organizations to include language in their articles of incorporation or bylaws that provide for indemnification of officers and directors charged with misconduct. Furthermore, directors' and officers' liability insurance or association professional liability insurance offer additional measures of protection.

Four Basic Financial Duties. All academic governing boards have four overarching financial responsibilities:

• *Maintain equity between generations.* Trustees have a responsibility to current students as well as students who will be enrolled in the future. Therefore, trustees must maintain the physical and financial assets of the institution, establish endowment-spending policies that preserve its purchasing power, and ensure that the institution's physical plant—its buildings, grounds, and equipment—is properly maintained.

• *Monitor strategic planning.* Strategic planning is fundamental to financial oversight. It gives trustees context within which to evaluate financial results. A strategic plan also enables boards to discuss priorities and make resource-allocation decisions. To be effective, institutional leaders must monitor the strategic plan and make sure it is updated regularly and when circumstances require it. Monitoring a strategic plan helps keep the board and senior management focused on important, long-term issues.

• *Establish financial controls.* The board is responsible for ensuring that adequate financial controls are in place. The audit committee, a standing board committee, is responsible for ensuring that financial record keeping and reporting are carried out in accordance with generally accepted accounting principles. The committee also ensures that independent audits of the institution's books and records occur and that a compliance review of relevant laws and contractual commitments takes place. Such financial controls enable boards to be confident that the financial reports they receive are accurate and reports to the general public are correct.

• *Manage risk.* Trustees should ensure their institutions are protected against catastrophic loss. Adequate property and casualty insurance must be in place, and the administration must develop policies covering the wide range of matters that can lead to lawsuits.

Current Reality. Fiduciary effectiveness flows from an understanding of the institution's "current reality." Is the institution in a strong position, or is it struggling? Are revenue sources strong or weak? Are expenses under control? Is the institution's capacity to attract prospective students increasing, decreasing, or holding steady? Are its leaders and managers effective and able? What is the institution's competitive position? Is it improving or eroding? Did it have an operating surplus or loss last year?

Various financial statements and reports should provide answers, but if a financial report is incomprehensible, trustees can ask the chief financial officer (CFO) to explain it in terms they can grasp.

The CFO undoubtedly will review with the board the Statement of Activities contained in the institution's most recent audited financial statements. This statement provides aggregated information about the revenues, expenses, and other sources of funds of the institution. It provides information on four critical end-of-year results trustees should monitor: (1) overall revenue and expenses, (2) operations, (3) investment performance, and (4) fund-raising.

The sample Statement of Activities that appears on page 8 illustrates basic financial information about a hypothetical university. (It is taken from the AGB book *Understanding Financial Statements*, by John H. McCarthy and Robert M. Turner, with Sandra L. Johnson, editor.) For the overall financial results for the fiscal year, look at the last line on the Statement of Activities, "Net assets at end of year." It shows that the university's net assets increased by $23,850,000 (7.5 percent) from

$317,563,000 in 1999 to $341,413,000 in 2000. Obviously, an increase in net assets is positive.

A trustee may want to ask the CFO a few questions: Where did the increase come from—operating surpluses, growth in the endowment, or gifts? Is the increase in net assets keeping up with the increase in inflation?

To find out whether the institution had a surplus from operations, check the middle of the statement for the line, "Increase in net assets from operating activities." This line shows the university had a net increase of $6,252,000. Revenues were $72,992,000, and expenses were $66,740,000. The university appeared to be living within its means. An inquisitive trustee will want to understand the reasons for an operating surplus (or deficit) and learn more about the sources and uses of the institution's revenue. How is the institution funded? Have there been any significant changes in its revenue sources? The CFO will elaborate the institution's current and future financial vulnerabilities, the stability of revenue sources, and the prospects for revenue growth. Questions such as these can contribute to useful conversations:

• Did anticipated and budgeted revenue match revenues actually received?

• Have revenue sources changed over the years, or have they been fairly constant?

• Has the institution had a bond issue in recent years to provide funds for one or more building projects? What was its bond rating? What would be the rating today?

• How dependent is the institution on any particular source of revenue?

• In which financial area is the institution most vulnerable?

In addition to the Statement of Activities, two types of documents provide excellent overviews:

• *Self-study reports needed for reaccreditations.* Every ten years, colleges and universities must undergo a reaccreditation process, part of which is an institutional self-study, for the regional accrediting organization. The self-study addresses a variety of "standards," which are used to assess such elements as academic programs, residential life, the condition of the campus, its financial standing, admissions strength, and service to the community. The resulting report provides a comprehensive overview of the institution, all in one place.

• *Offering statement for selling the institution's bonds.* Many institutions issue debt and are required to prepare documents for bondholders and bond-rating agencies. The offering statement in these documents provides a concise overview of the institution's financial condition.

Understanding an institution's vulnerabilities is a key component of the fiduciary thought process. It provides a dash of reality and helps define areas that need to be monitored. It also prompts campus leaders to view their institution in a realistic light.

After a trustee understands revenue sources, the next step is to examine

STATEMENT OF ACTIVITIES
FOR THE YEARS ENDED JUNE 30, 2000 AND 1999 (IN THOUSANDS)

	Unrestricted	Temporarily Restricted	Permanently Restricted	2000 Total	1999 Total
Operating Revenues					
Tuition and fees	$54,298			$54,298	$49,077
University sponsored financial aid	(5,145)			(5,145)	(4,446)
Donor sponsored financial aid	(9,988)			(9,988)	(8,892)
Net tuition and fees	39,165			39,165	35,739
Sales and services of auxiliaries	12,099			12,099	10,628
Government grants and contracts	1,991			1,991	1,684
Private gifts and grants	4,084	2,639		6,723	5,647
Long-term investment income	4,110	4,943		9,053	10,152
Investment gains used for operations	1,191	1,456		2,647	963
Other income	1,314			1,314	1,285
Net assets released form restrictions	6,266	(6,266)			
Total operating revenues	70,220	2,772		72,992	66,098
Operating Expenses					
Instruction and research	27,619			27,619	25,783
Athletics	6,001			6,001	5,499
Academic support	6,367			6,367	6,321
Student services	6,085			6,085	5,643
Institutional support	10,648			10,648	10,472
Auxiliary enterprises	10,020			10,020	8,845
Total operating expenses	66,740			66,740	62,563
Increase in net assets from operating activities	3,840	2,772		6,252	3,535
Nonoperating Activities					
Investment gains reinvested	5,024	8,174		13,198	1,793
Capital gifts	934	1,921	3,965	6,820	8,511
Other	(1,197)	(1,223)		(2,420)	(969)
Net assets released from restrictions	1,629	(1,629)			
Increase in net assets from nonoperating activities	6,390	7,234	3,965	17,598	9,335
Net increase in net assets for the year before change in accounting	9,870	10,015	3,965	23,850	12,870
Effects of changes in acounting:					
Contribution pledged					15,285
Postretirement benefits					(5,645)
Net increase in net assets	9,879	10,015	3.965	23,850	22,510
Net assets at beginning of year	147,342	93,522	76,699	317,563	295,052
Net assets at end of year	$157,212	$103,537	$80,664	$341,413	$317,562

institutional spending. Where does the money go? Once again, trustees should turn to the Statement of Activities for a list of operating expenses broken down into broad categories. In the sample statement on page 8, the first line under the heading "Operating Expenses" shows that the university spent $27,619,000, or 41 percent, of its operating revenues on "Instruction and research." Most institutions want this to be their largest expense area because that is the core business. Included in this expense category are all faculty and research salaries, equipment used for teaching and research, and the cost of running departments closely related to the teaching function. More difficult to ascertain is whether the institution spends *sufficient* funds on instruction and whether those funds are spent effectively. Trustees will want to understand each major category of expense and the rate of growth for each category.

As fiduciaries, trustees should understand what drives the growth rate of expenses from one year to another. The CFO can answer this question, but the explanation will be complex. Most institutions are experiencing increasing payroll costs without corresponding increases in "productivity." Also driving expenses are state-of-the-art computing facilities; deferred maintenance costs; increasing demand for more and better student services; expanding fields of knowledge that have increased the size, scope, and breadth of the curriculum; and internal issues that make it difficult to cut academic programs.

The sample Statement o also provides a snapshot of th ment returns of the endowmen CFO probably will provide more   ..is on the endowment's performance, but an analysis of several lines of the statement enables a quick calculation of the total return of the endowment. For example, the heading "Operating Revenues" shows that $9,053,000 of

As fiduciaries, trustees should understand what drives the growth rate of expenses from one year to another.

"Long-term investment income" was used to support the operating budget. Also, $2,647,000 of "Investment gains" was used for operations. Under the heading "Nonoperating Activities," the line "Investment gains reinvested" shows unrealized gains of $13,198,000. Consequently, it is possible to calculate the total return of the endowment for the year by adding together the interest and dividends, and the realized and unrealized gains. On the sample statement: $9,053,000 + $2,647,000 + $13,198,000 = $24,898,000. The average market value of the endowment for the year was $244,989,000. Thus, the total return on the endowment was 10.1 percent ($244,989,000 ÷ $24,898,000 = 10.1 percent).

Trustees should be interested in the amount and number of gifts to the institution. Under the heading "Operating Revenues," the sample statement has a line, "Private gifts and grants." It shows the university raised a total of $6,723,000 during the year. Trustees will want to know the breakdown between restricted and unrestricted gifts that support the operating budget. Also, gifts designated for the endowment or for capital projects can be found under the heading "Nonoperating Activities." The line "Capital gifts" shows that these gifts amounted to $6,820,000.Trustees will want more information on giving patterns, trends, and the cost of raising funds. For many institutions, attracting unrestricted gifts is essential to balancing the operating budget.

Sustainability. This is a fiduciary concept that refers to the sustainability of resources—from tuition, the endowment, government grants, or gifts. A balanced operating budget is critical, as is the reliability of the sources of revenue over time. A responsible fiduciary

An institutional goal to maintain the status quo probably signals trouble.

would not be satisfied with a report that the institution had a good year. It is important to know why. Are current income streams sustainable? What level of income can the institution depend on year after year? When income is not stable and fluctuates from year to year,

reserves provide an important cushion.

The board should strive to match sustainable income with the institution's basic mission and ensure institutional goals are consistent with the resources needed to finance them. If a large percentage of the institution's income is highly variable, a program should be built around the most predictable, sustainable income sources with provisions for augmenting the program when the variable income is known. Nothing is certain, of course, but a pattern of revenue income that is consistent over time can be considered sustainable. Trend and ratio data are important concepts that are addressed in detail later in this book.

Financial Flexibility. In addition to matching sustainable income to the core mission of the institution, trustees should be mindful of opportunities for growth and innovation. An institutional goal to maintain the status quo probably signals trouble. If most of an institution's expenses are in fixed costs (a very common reality), campus officials have little opportunity to support innovation. Consequently, institutional leaders must raise funds for innovation and improvement from external sources through targeted individual gifts or contributions to the endowment.

It is difficult for institutional leaders or faculty members to sustain the energy required for new initiatives when support is uncertain. Many promising innovations wither for lack of adequate, sustained funding. For these reasons, and to "invest" in the long-term improvement of the institution, a trustee who is a good fiduciary supports the concept of financial flexibility. Without it, an institution may lack the capacity to change and to maintain a vibrant and responsive educational community.

For institutions whose "current reality" is simple survival, the suggestion that funds be set aside for innovation or for new programs may seem ludicrous. However, if contingency funds for innovation come at the end of the resource-allocation decision process, innovation rarely will be funded. Prudent planning requires that appropriate levels of reserves be allocated as part of the budget process.

Intergenerational Equity. Trustees are responsible for maintaining equity between current and future students. They must have a long-term perspective and be concerned equally for currently enrolled students, those who may enter in the next few years, and for students not yet born. Higher education institutions should be managed and sustained in perpetuity.

To maintain intergenerational equity, trustees must ensure that physical and financial assets are consumed at a rate that enables them to be replenished for the next generation. This requires that they oversee an endowment-spending policy that maintains the endowment's purchasing power. Similarly, they must ensure buildings and equipment are maintained and replenished for each generation of students.

It is common for imbalances to occur for short periods of time. A college may incur deficits during an especially difficult time, or it may fall behind in its maintenance of buildings and grounds. On the flip side, during strong bull markets and periods that yield above-average endowment returns, a college may save more surplus funds for future students than it spends on current students. This balancing act is imprecise; maintaining equilibrium between the present and the future is not easy. Trustees should carefully monitor the use of financial and physical resources and remain mindful of their commitment to ensure intergenerational equity.

Financial Equilibrium. Intergenerational equity and financial equilibrium are closely linked. Financial equilibrium is elusive—hard to reach and even harder to sustain—but it is an important goal. For an institution to be in financial equilibrium, it must maintain four conditions simultaneously:

1. *Operating budgets are balanced.* Income and expenses should be in balance, and there should be an appropriate match between sources of revenue and the uses to which they are put. That is, long-term uses of revenue should be supported by long-term sources of capital; short-term uses should be funded by short-term sources. An institution should not balance its operating budget by long-term debt financing or fund major capital projects through short-term borrowing.

2. *Physical assets are preserved.* One of an institution's major financial concerns is to maintain the useful life of its physical assets. How much should an institution spend annually on such costs? This difficult question is addressed in more depth in Chapter 6, but a good approximation can be found in an annual depreciation calculation. To be in financial equilibrium, an institution must fully fund depreciation in the annual operating budget.

3. *The endowment's purchasing power is protected.* Consider this general guideline to maintain an endowment's purchasing power: The amount taken from the endowment to support annual operations, plus a factor for the rate of inflation, should equal the total return of the endowment. For example, if a college annually draws 5 percent of the market value of the endowment and inflation is 3 percent, the total return for the endowment should be 8 percent, after investment fees. However, endowments do not grow in such neat, linear patterns, so most institutions use a spending formula that averages and smoothes for market fluctuations over a three-year period.

4. *Human assets are developed and nourished.* Faculty and staff are an institution's most important assets. Salaries and benefits must remain competitive, and individuals must have opportunities for professional development—or the best faculty and staff members will become demoralized or leave. Maintaining the human side of the enterprise also means providing periodic sabbaticals for key faculty and staff members.

Although few institutions find financial equilibrium, these four conditions are important to attain. When trustees review annual operating budgets and financial statements, they should assess their institution's proximity to financial equilibrium and discuss what actions are required to achieve it. Institutions that fall short will remain in a constant state of financial stress, which inevitably causes other tensions.

Basic Consumer Questions. All trustees should have a basic understanding of certain economic facts about their institutions. The ability to think like a consumer—that is, to understand the economic reality of students attending their institution—is important. Trustees should be able to answer some basic consumer questions, such as the following:

• What is our annual tuition, and how does it compare with that of our competitors in the public and private sectors?

• What other institutions constitute a peer group for the purposes of comparison and benchmarking?

• What is the total cost for a full-paying student to receive a degree?

• What is the average loan burden of a student upon graduation?

• What percentage of students receive financial aid?

• What is the size of the average scholarship package?

• What percentage of financial need cannot be met?

• What is the true cost of educating a student at our school?

• What are the institution's "expensive policies"? These policies are not required but often are part of the institution's value system. For example, consciously setting a low student-faculty ratio of, say, ten students to one faculty member. What do such policies cost, either in funds or as a percentage of budgets? How have they changed in the last five years, and how are they likely to change in the next five? (For more about this concept, see Chapter 7.)

• Are the expensive policies aligned with the institution's mission, values, and strategic objectives?

Summary. Thinking like a fiduciary begins with a conscious effort to understand the institution's economics. This process becomes intuitive as trustees grow accustomed to understanding data, asking focused questions, and developing policies that guide the institution. At its core, fiduciary thinking requires trustees to have a sense of institutional ownership, a dedication to current and future students, and a commitment to address current financial issues and plan for those of the future.

The fiduciary thought process requires that trustees understand where the institution may be vulnerable and to seek ways to sustain revenue sources. Financial equilibrium and financial flexibility are highly desirable priorities. Colleges and universities need trustees who can ask challenging and fair questions, avoid dysfunctional politeness, deal with facts and data, and appreciate the complexities of running an education institution.

Colleges and universities have particularly complex cultures. If trustees are to exercise their financial responsibilities effectively, they need to invest time, thought, and attention to the culture, values, and governance structures of their institutions. They need to be politically attuned to the limits of power inherent in academic governance structures where institutional values change very slowly. The board's ultimate leadership is best exercised through careful decisions regarding how and where to spend the institution's limited resources over time. And this requires good strategic planning.

Recommended Readings

"The Attorney General's Guide for Board Members of Charitable Organizations," by Scott Harshbarger. Commonwealth of Massachusetts, 1997.

Board Basics: "AGB Statement on Institutional Governance." AGB, 1998.

Board Basics: "Financial Responsibilities," by Tracy J. Burlock and Kent John Chabotar. AGB, 1998.

Board Basics: "Institutional Ethics and Values," by Thomas E. Corts. AGB, 1998.

Board Basics: "Trustee Responsibilities: A Guide for Governing Boards of Public [Private] Institutions," by Richard T. Ingram. AGB, 1997.

College and University Business Administration, Sixth Edition. NACUBO, 2000.

College and Universities Foundations: Serving America's Public Higher Education, edited by Joseph Phelan. AGB, 1997.

The Effective Board of Trustees, by Richard P. Chait, Thomas P. Holland, and Barbara E. Taylor. American Council on Education and Oryx Press, 1993.

How Academic Leadership Works— Understanding Success and Failure in the College Presidency, by Robert Birnbaum. Jossey-Bass Publishers, 1992.

How Colleges Work—The Cybernetics of Academic Organization and Leadership, by Robert Birnbaum. National Center for Postsecondary Governance and Finance, 1991.

Inside the Boardroom: Governance by Directors and Trustees, by William G. Bowen. John Wiley & Sons, Inc. 1994.

Managing the Nonprofit Organization, by Peter Drucker. Harper Business, 1990.

Once Upon a Campus—Lessons for Improving Quality and Productivity in Higher Education, by Daniel Seymour. American Council on Education, Oryx Press, 1995.

"The Role of the Board," by Richard P. Chait in *Strategy and Finance in Higher Education*, William F. Massy and Joel W. Myerson, editors. Peterson's, 1994.

"Walking the Trustee Tightrope," by William S. Reed, in *Trusteeship*, AGB, January/February 1993.

What Every Trustee Should Know: A Manual for Trustees of Independent Colleges and Universities, by Robert D. Peck and the President's Foundation for the Support of Higher Education, 1995.

The University—An Owner's Manual, by Henry Rosovky. W.W. Norton & Company, 1990.

CHAPTER 2

Conducting
A Workable
Budgeting Process

Trustees who hope to contribute in meaningful ways to sound resource-allocation decisions must know how their institutions develop and construct operating budgets. Operating budgets contain countless details and do not change significantly from year to year, given that they contain substantial fixed costs. Although "discretionary funds" typically constitute a small portion of the budget, trustees should ask two essential questions when the budget is placed before the board for review and approval: (1) Is the institution spending its money in accordance with its mission and core values? (2) Does this budget move the institution closer to or away from financial equilibrium?

At all colleges and universities, requests for funds far exceed available resources. Academic leaders, with the board, must select what to fund and what not to fund. In fact, the options an institution chooses not to fund are as declarative of values, culture, and mission as those that are funded.

Reviewing and approving annual operating budgets are central to board control and influence. If a board simply approves budgets without engaging in informed discussions, it is doing itself and the institution a disservice. At the same time, however, every board must determine its appropriate degree of involvement in the budget process, with and through the finance committee. Clearly, boards should help set basic parameters, financial principles, and overall guidelines, and they should ask probing questions about trends, priorities, and pressures. However, unless an institution is in a financial crisis, the board should resist becoming involved in budget decisions at the department or line-item level.

The Budget Process Reflects Institutional Culture. Sound budget processes reflect an institution's culture, traditions, and governance structure. They also should be sufficiently flexible to reflect institutional change and be responsive to new fiscal realities. In the final analysis, the budget process is as much about setting institutional priorities as it is about control and accountability.

Three basic methods for developing budgets dominate higher education finance:

• *Highly centralized*. This is an efficient process that relies on constituents having a high level of trust in the central administration. This process is used most frequently when an institution has weak or inconsistent faculty participation in decision making or when the institution is at risk financially. At institutions that use this process, faculty advisory committees often collaborate with administrators to resolve difficult issues concerning priorities among departments competing for the same resources.

• *Decentralized*. This process places control and accountability in departments or schools. Decentralized units are responsible for generating their own revenue and controlling their own expenses; thus, budget development may differ significantly among departments and schools. The central administration puts the pieces together, establishes rules for common policies and expenses (such as fringe benefits and tuition rates), and sets an overhead charge to pay for central services.

• *Broad based*. This process is common at small or decentralized institutions with strong traditions of shared governance. Some major research universities have highly sophisticated budget

processes in which stakeholders are actively engaged. Committees of faculty, administrators, staff, and students work throughout the year to create a balanced budget, which they present to the provost and/or president for review, approval, and subsequent review and discussion by the board's finance committee and the board itself. Other institutions may have budget advisory committees that discuss priorities and keep the broader campus community informed about resource-allocation decisions.

The budget process is as much about setting institutional priorities as it is about control and accountability.

There is no "correct" way to develop a budget. These approaches are not mutually exclusive, and aspects of all three overlap at most institutions. Depending on circumstances, any one of the processes could be the most effective approach for an institution at any given time. However, if the budget process contradicts institutional culture (when an institution that prizes collaborative governance and consultation employs a highly centralized budget process, for example), the board can expect discontent. Recovering from such situations often is difficult.

Developing Budgetary Guidelines and Financial Principles. Governing board leadership calls for the development of a set of financial principles that guide the budget process. Financial principles are crucial to long-range planning and to the annual operating budget. They are a blueprint for implementing strategic goals and protecting the institution's financial equilibrium.

Consider this example, which illustrates how a liberal arts college developed financial principles in response to a problem common among independent institutions:

A long-range projection showed that operating deficits would occur in five years unless officials used the most optimistic assumptions for projecting endowment growth rates. An ad-hoc committee of trustees, faculty, and staff was convened to carry out two important tasks. First, it would reexamine the financial assumptions and benchmarks established by a previously established committee. Second, it would recommend to the board a set of financial principles that would meet the institution's long-term objectives of (1) allocating resources efficiently and effectively to reflect the college's values and priorities and (2) operating in financial equilibrium. This ad-hoc committee developed a set of financial principles designed to return the college to financial equilibrium within five years. The principles addressed these elements:

• *College size.* The committee established a target goal for student full-time equivalent (FTE) for each of the next five years.

• *Tuition growth.* It set a specific cap for tuition growth. The institution committed to an annual analysis of tuition growth compared with that of peer institutions.

• *Staffing levels.* The committee developed a plan to reduce the number of staff not directly related to teaching. Targets were established for each area of the college, and an early retirement program was put in place.

• *Endowment spending rate.* The committee recommended a new way of calculating endowment spending to preserve the endowment's long-term purchasing power. Further, it set specific guidelines for the endowment's contribution to the educational and general (E & G) budget. (Educational and general expenses include all of the costs of running the institution with the exception of "auxiliary enterprises," which are the costs related to room and board and other noneducational functions, such as the bookstore.)

• *Gift support.* The committee established specific fund-raising targets for the annual operating budget and the endowment. The goal for raising unrestricted funds was tagged to a specific percentage of E&G revenues.

• *Financial aid.* The institution recommitted itself to maintain its need-blind admissions policy and to fully fund financial aid for students who needed it. The committee decided to continue this policy unless costs climbed above a certain threshold and triggered a review.

• *Salary objectives.* Noting that faculty and staff salaries had slipped behind those at peer institutions, the committee declared its intention to return salaries to their former ranking and established salary targets for administrative and support staff.

   • *Major maintenance.* To comply with FASB accounting standards, the college decided to fully fund depreciation within the operating budget. Realizing this would put the budget out of balance, the goal was to fully incorporate depreciation in the operating budget within five years.

   • *Debt financing for capital projects.* An important issue for the board was its debt policy. Should the college finance some major renovation projects through debt financing? The committee set specific guidelines to determine when to issue additional debt, making certain to protect the college's favorable credit rating.

   • *Innovation fund.* To ensure flexibility for innovation or experimentation in future budgets, the committee recommended that some revenue should be reserved every year in an innovation fund.

Influencing the Budget Process. The administration is responsible for putting the budget together and managing it throughout the year. Trustees are not responsible for managing the process; rather, they influence the process at appropriate levels and times. The questions for trustees are "Where?" and "When?"

   It is common practice for four board committees to be involved directly and indirectly in developing annual operating budgets: the finance committee

(often called the budget committee), the buildings and grounds committee, the investment committee, and the development committee. These committees have other responsibilities, of course, but their budget-related responsibilities are briefly described here:

   • *The Finance (or Budget) Committee.* The finance or budget committee's primary responsibilities are to ensure the fiscal stability and long-term economic health of the institution. Finance committees may concentrate on different issues, depending on the economic health or the mission of the institution. For example, at research institutions, finance committee members must understand the complexity of research funding and indirect-cost recovery. At comprehensive four-year institutions, committee members must understand their institution's academic focus. And at community colleges, committee members must understand the importance their colleges place on cost-effective delivery of credit hours. Regardless of the unique circumstances of each institution, all finance committees must review the assumptions that underlie budget development, set broad guidelines, review budget priorities, and analyze trends and long-range financial projections.

   The finance committee's responsibility is to bring to life the institution's mission, for nothing happens without funding. During the resource-allocation process, the operating budget becomes the key tool for implementing decisions. The finance committee must address the critical issues of tuition and financial aid, the cost of delivering the educational product, the amount to invest to maintain the physical plant, the compensation objectives for faculty and staff, and how much of endowment income to spend on current operations. The finance committee must ensure not only that the budget is balanced but also that the budget meets the institution's strategic objectives. Because the finance committee's charge is so broad and so critical to fulfilling the institution's mission, every trustee should serve on this committee sometime during his or her board service. Doing so is an excellent way to learn how the institution really works.

• *The Buildings and Grounds (or Facilities) Committee.* This committee is responsible for determining the amount of major maintenance required on campus—a budget item that can be substantial because there always are a greater number of maintenance projects than can be funded in any given year. This committee also makes judgments about renewal and renovation projects that fall into the gray area between expensed projects and capital projects. When considering these projects, committee members should pose two key questions: Will the project under consideration maintain or extend the useful life of a building? How much money will the project require? Capital projects (new construction) are not included in the operating budget but are part of the capital budget. (See Chapter 6.)

In general, committee members should keep in mind that about 1.5 percent to 3 percent of the physical plant's replacement value should be funded annually for major maintenance. This calculation, however, is more art than science. The usual methodology is to categorize the buildings by type— dormitory, classroom, office space, wet laboratory, athletic facilities, and so on— and multiply the square footage for each

Persistent deferred maintenance inevitably leads to major crises.

category by prevailing construction cost.

The 1.5 percent-to-3 percent range is a judgment call that depends on a building's age, architecture, and degree of maintenance required. If a campus has been adequately maintained over time, 1.5 percent of replacement value may be sufficient. A campus that has fallen behind in major maintenance might require a 3 percent investment. Many institutions conduct periodic assessments of their physical plant to develop a rolling major maintenance schedule to ensure the institution's facilities are cared for adequately.

Too often, however, institutional leaders and boards decide to cut badly needed maintenance projects to balance the operating budget. Persistent deferred maintenance inevitably leads to major crises. Trustees are responsible for ensuring the campus's physical assets are maintained properly. Doing so is a fundamental fiduciary responsibility, and the temptation to defer maintenance should be resisted.

At some institutions, the buildings and grounds committee also is responsible for overseeing information-technology policies, especially those regarding such infrastructure needs as new computer labs and dormitory connections to the Internet. Clearly, these responsibilities have substantial budget implications.

• *The Investment Committee.* This committee is responsible for setting endowment spending guidelines. For many institutions, endowments provide important revenue. One obvious way to balance an operating budget is to spend more from the endowment fund. This practice is tempting, especially when investment returns are high. Boards should establish written policy guidelines to preserve the purchasing power of the endowment while providing an appropriate contribution to the operating budget. This is known as the "endowment spending rate."

Institutions use a variety of methods to calculate appropriate endowment spending rates. Whatever the method used, the objective in setting the rate should be to smooth out the amount available each year—to minimize large swings from one year to the next. The most common method, known as "total return," averages the market value of the endowment over a trailing three years and applies a percentage (usually around 5 percent) to that average. This method is conservative because the trailing three-year average usually is lower than the year-end average, unless there is a sustained bear market. Some institutions spend only the interest, div-

idends, and rental income from their endowment investments.

Another approach is to separate the endowment's performance from the spending calculation. With this approach, the endowment's contribution to operating revenue is increased by a specified percentage over the previous year. For instance, the increase may be the current rate of inflation. If inflation for the preceding fiscal year were 3 percent, the endowment's contribution to the operating budget would be 103 percent of the preceding year's amount.

Spending rate formulas can range from quite simple to very complicated. What's important is that over time the board must maintain the endowment's purchasing power to preserve intergenerational equity.

• *The Development Committee.* The development committee, sometimes called the institutional advancement committee, sets annual fund-raising goals and participates in the process of determining short-term and long-term fund-raising projects, including comprehensive campaigns. Committee members set policy guidelines, participate in activities that support policy implementation, understand that they are expected to make personal contributions, and are involved in soliciting other trustees or major gift prospects.

The committee's work varies from year to year. During periods when the institution is not engaged in a comprehensive campaign, the committee may attend to strengthening or expanding the capabilities of the development staff,

All trustees should understand the financial implications of fund-raising objectives.

planning the next campaign, providing development staff members with suggestions and contacts, overseeing stewardship issues, supporting the annual-giving program, and monitoring the flow of gifts.

The development committee is responsible for establishing and monitoring several important policies. Its members will consider many questions: What size of gift is required to establish an endowed fund or to endow a professorship or a scholarship? How will gifts of property and real estate be credited and disposed of? Should naming opportunities have a strict dollar amount (a percentage of the building's cost, for example), or should such matters be negotiated case by case? Should the institution recognize gifts by level (the President's Club, for example, or an Alumni Club)? Do individuals receive credit for corporate matching gifts?

The list of policy issues is broad and sometimes politically sensitive. Resolving them is critical to a successful development program. Establishing fund-raising goals is a delicate process that requires matching institutional needs with a realistic assessment of donors' interests, readiness, and capacities. What's more, fund-raising goals affect budget decisions and institutional priorities and should be set in conjunction with the finance and buildings and grounds committees.

All trustees should understand the financial implications of fund-raising objectives. How much is for budget relief, and how much supports new programs? Will new programs be self-sustaining, or will the operating budget absorb additional costs to provide ongoing support for them? Fund-raising objectives should mirror strategic objectives and lessen the financial load on the operating budget. A gift always should leave the institution in a stronger financial position, not a weaker one. If the institution's operating budget ultimately must absorb additional costs because of the gift—either through additional operating costs, sustaining a new program, or supporting a new building—the board should be assured that the benefits of the gift outweigh the costs.

• *The Audit Committee.* The audit committee's primary responsibility is to oversee the work of the financial officers of the institution as well as its internal and independent auditors. This involves understanding and monitoring the institution's risk management and its compliance with regulations and laws. The committee is not a policymaking body; rather, it ensures that policies are carried out. In doing so, committee members must rely on information supplied by the senior financial officers of the college and independent auditors. (For more about audit committee responsibilities see Chapter 8.)

• *Other Committees.* To lesser degrees,

the academic affairs committee (which addresses issues of academic program development and faculty personnel and compensation issues) and the student-affairs committee are involved in some components of budget development. Furthermore, governing boards may choose to organize ad-hoc committees to address special or high-cost needs, such as information technology. During times of fiscal crisis, an entire board often will become involved in developing the institution's annual operating budget.

Different Approaches to Budgeting. Just as there are various ways for an academic community to be involved in the budget process, there are various approaches to budgeting. Six are common. While they share some features, each has a distinct focus and relies on different kinds of information.

• *Incremental budgeting*. Incremental budgeting often is referred to as "cost plus" budgeting because it is merely the process of increasing last year's budget by the rate of inflation or another factor. It requires little thought, and it assumes and protects the status quo. It may reflect marginal change, but it rarely reflects numerous or fundamental changes.

Incremental budgeting is the most common budgeting process in higher education for several reasons: Most colleges and universities have a high proportion of fixed costs; their academic priorities and curricula do not vary greatly from year to year; and existing programs usually are funded. Incremental budgeting is efficient,

relatively easy to carry out, and favored from a political standpoint because it minimizes conflict and surprise.

But this process assumes that the budget base reflects appropriate resource allocations. Because few funds are available for new programs or initiatives, fewer hard choices must be made. From time to time, institutional leaders may decide to increase salaries to catch up to the competition, decrease deferred maintenance, or slow the growth of personnel expenses. But these adjustments are just that—marginal adjustments to the base budget, not changes driven by data or an analytical assessment of needs and requirements for the long term.

• *Planning, Programming, and Budgeting Systems (PPBS)*. PPBS is the antithesis of incremental budgeting. It makes a great deal of sense in theory, but it is very difficult to implement. It attempts to link planning to resource allocation. It examines the costs of programs and measures them according to the degree to which they advance the institution's mission and goals. It requires a highly centralized approach to budget development, sophisticated information systems, and a capacity for quantitative analysis. It also requires institutional leaders to set clear objectives and goals and determine ways to evaluate them using objective analysis.

Subsequently, budget and academic officers must conduct a rigorous quantitative analysis of policy alternatives to determine where to invest institutional resources to receive the best return on a cost-benefit basis. They must make long-term projections on program costs and outputs to weigh policy alternatives and to predict the fiscal implications of policy decisions.

Few academic institutions have adopted this complicated approach, mostly because they lack the methodology to evaluate program benefits and determine true costs. This approach, however, may gain favor, especially as institutions are compelled to justify tuition increases on a cost-benefit basis.

• *Zero-based budgeting*. This approach is the other side of the budgeting coin. It assumes no budget history; each year is a new beginning. Departments and budget units annually must justify their programs and activities anew by outlining the benefits and arguing the consequences of not conducting them. Zero-based budgeting is a time-consuming process and may create more work than the results justify.

Additionally, it is unrealistic to assume that major programs will not continue from year to year, so a zero-based budget process really does not start from zero. For most institutions, the budget process starts at about 80 percent of the previous year's budget. Departments are required to justify only 20 percent of their budgets. Especially when an institution is in fiscal crisis, some elements of zero-based budgeting can help determine where cuts may be made.

• *Performance budgeting*. Primarily used by public institutions, this approach is aimed at improving efficiency by relating resources (inputs) to activities (structure) and results (outputs). Several states have adopted performance-budgeting approaches, although the standards most often affect only very small portions of institutional budgets. Usually, the process is controlled centrally, with performance standards set by state legislatures or other state agencies. In some states, the standards are used as incentives for institutions to comply with the state's public agenda.

This approach requires a great deal of quantitative analysis, and it generates voluminous paperwork. Those who favor performance budgeting contend it is an important step toward greater accountability and compels colleges and universities to address cost containment more systematically. Those who disagree say that performance is not measured accurately and the approach is too simplistic. Whether performance budgeting is a fad or a trend remains to be seen.

• *Formula budgeting*. Public institutions that operate within centralized systemwide budget processes employ this method. It allocates resources based on the relationship between program demand and program cost. It is mathematically driven, using simple ratios (student-to-faculty ratios or the number of square feet to be maintained) or more complex ratios (the cost per student credit hour by discipline, for example). This approach attempts to make resource-allocation decisions on a rational basis by relying on mathematics and removing politics from the process. However, the formula always is open for debate. Critics of formula budgeting contend that it does not encourage excellence or experimentation.

Almost all budget-development approaches incorporate elements of formula budgeting. When governing boards establish budget guidelines, they are using a modified version of formula budgeting. Declarations that tuition cannot rise faster than inflation, salary increases shall be the average of peer institutions, or the endowment spending rate shall not exceed 5 percent of a trailing three-year average are examples of modified versions of formula budgeting.

• *Responsibility-center budgeting.* Most major, independent research universities employ some form of responsibility-center budgeting. Harvard University is well known for its "every tub on its own bottom" management approach. It decentralizes the responsibility for resource management to colleges, schools, and departments, which become individual revenue and cost centers.

Responsibility-center budgeting is based on a calculation of each unit's total revenues and costs, plus an indirect charge for services provided by the central administration. This type of budgeting assumes that surpluses will be carried forward from one year to the next and that deficits will be carried forward as liabilities against future budgets. Under this system, the central administration acts as a holding company, and the individual schools are responsible for their own performance and outcomes.

This approach requires the central administration to "sell" its services to the schools at a price and quality that are competitive with the commercial world—a concept that can create tension between the broader mission of the university and the particular mission of a school or college.

Another potential source of tension may arise in the case of "wealthy" schools versus "poor" schools, particularly when the "poor" school is crucial to the institution's core mission. Students may have very different experiences depending on whether they are enrolled in a wealthy school or one that is financially strapped. For this approach to work well, all schools must share a sense of the institution's overall mission, be willing to compromise for the good of the whole, and coordinate vital areas such as fund-raising, financial-aid, and accounting protocols.

Budget methodology should give trustees a great deal of information about the institution's culture, governance structure, accountability, and controls. No single methodology is "right." The best approach depends on the institution's circumstances and needs, and incorporating elements of more than one approach to budgeting often makes sense.

The Budget Cycle. Methodologies may differ among institutions, but most have similar budget cycles. Usually, the budget cycle is geared to the board's meeting schedule to facilitate various approvals and to help set tuition in time to inform newly admitted students. A typical budget cycle has four stages:

• *Early fall*. Budget officers review the previous year's budget performance and long-range assumptions and determine whether any developments at the institution will affect the next budget.

• *Late fall and early winter*. Budget officers reaffirm or adjust budget guidelines, review priorities, and send guidelines and budget instructions to departments.

• *Mid and late winter*. Departments develop budgets and submit them to the administration for review. The administration sets revenue objectives from tuition, endowment, gifts, and sponsored research. Many meetings occur to match revenues with expenses.

• *Spring*. Budget officers construct the final budget and submit it to the finance or budget committee and the full board for review and approval. After approval, institutional officers inform departments of their budget for the next year, students of tuition and financial aid, and staff of salary and performance-review schedules.

Public institutions and systems have a much more complicated process, of course. But the point is that both independent college and university boards need to be articulate about the process and the results. They should be able to explain and defend, if necessary, the proposed budgets for the subsequent fiscal year.

Budget Assumptions. Budgets are built around a set of assumptions about the future that underpin an institution's long-range plan. As a starting point, the annual operating budget tracks actual performance for the previous fiscal year and reviews the long-term planning assumptions. Both of these exercises are crucial to the institution's future well-being, and the board should be involved in them. Projections can be positive or negative, depending on the assumptions.

At least 15 critical assumptions influence the development of an academic budget. They are rate of inflation; size of student body; rates of growth for comprehensive fees, net tuition, tuition discounting, endowment return, annual gifts, payroll, non-personnel expenses, and computing and other capital expenses; indirect cost recovery; faculty-to-student ratio; faculty teaching load; major maintenance expenses; profitability of auxiliary enterprises; and the profitability of related activities, such as a hospital or an affiliated research center.

Each planning assumption will increase or decrease in importance depending on the type of institution. For a college that relies heavily on the earning power of a large endowment, a key assumption is the rate of endowment growth and its earnings. For an institution with a small endowment, this variable is less important. For major research universities, a crucial variable may be the indirect-cost recovery rate (the amount of funds an institution is reimbursed from externally sponsored research contracts for overhead expenses). For a teaching liberal arts college, such a variable would not be significant because government research grants typically are a small source of revenue.

Campus administrators should conduct a "sensitivity analysis" for each assumption to predict the effect of change. For example, a sensitivity analysis might show that every 1 percent increase in net tuition generates $1 million in extra revenue or that every 1 percent increase in salary adjustments adds $500,000 to the payroll.

Determining assumptions and conducting sensitivity analyses are important tasks for the administration. It is equally important for the board to be comfortable with the assumptions and analyses because these constitute the foundation on which the operating budget is built. It is vital that key institutional leaders agree on these critical assumptions.

Strategic Budgeting. Building an innovation fund into an annual budget is a good example of strategic budgeting. Quite simply, strategic budgeting involves funding high-priority strategic items first. More traditional budgeting involves making routine budget allocations first and then funding strategic initiatives. As a consequence, strategic initiatives are not funded or generally are funded through outside gifts. Strategic budgeting requires making hard choices about what to cut from other budget areas to fund innovations and to bring the budget into balance.

Core Budgeting. Boards can directly affect the budget process without micromanaging by implementing "core budgeting." This concept is simple in

theory but hard to implement because it requires consensus on "core activities." In general, the "core" is the institution's fixed costs plus the costs of essential programs.

More specifically, core budgeting works like this: Finance officers might budget revenues conservatively because they predict tuition or unrestricted-gift

Boards can directly affect the budget process without micromanaging.

revenue will be below target. Once they determine actual revenue—assuming it is greater than the conservative estimate on which the budget was built—the "excess revenue" is allocated to predetermined projects, which the institution deems important but not essential. This process can be helpful when revenues are volatile or when the institution wishes to discontinue incremental budgeting.

Summary. The board's oversight role in approving the budget is one of the most important financial responsibilities it exercises. It involves making decisions on the critical issue of tuition levels and financial aid, the cost of delivering the educational product, the amount to invest to maintain the physical plant, the compensation objectives for faculty and staff, and the determination of how much endowment income to spend on current operations.

In exercising this responsibility, the board normally works through the finance (budget) committee. The oversight of the budget, first and foremost, involves making certain the budget process reflects the institution's culture and mission. The finance committee, working with senior management, develops broad budgetary guidelines and financial principles and approves the assumptions on which the current budget and long-range projections are based.

Colleges and universities employ a variety of budget processes, ranging from highly centralized to decentralized. Just as there are various ways for an academic community to be involved in the budget process, there are various approaches to budgeting. Six are most common: incremental; planning, programming, and budgetary systems; zero-based; performance; formula; and responsibility-center budgeting. While all six share certain features, each has a distinct focus and relies on different kinds of information. Because the finance committee's responsibilities are so broad and closely linked to the institutional mission, every trustee should serve on this committee sometime during his or her board service.

Recommended Readings

Board Basics: "The Board's Role in Fund-Raising," by Richard D. Legon. AGB, 1997.

Board Basics: "The Buildings and Grounds Committee," by Ronald T. Flinn. AGB, 1997.

Board Basics: "The Finance Committee," by James E. Morley, Jr. AGB, 1997.

Board Basics: "Financial Responsibilities," by Tracy Burlock and Kent John Chabotar. AGB, 1998.

Board Basics: "The Investment Committee," by John H. Biggs. AGB, 1997.

"Budgeting: A Tool For Planning and Control," and "Zero-Based Budgeting and Program Budget," by J.K Shim and J.G. Siegel in *Financial Management of Nonprofits*. Irwin Professional Publishers, 1997.

College and University Budgeting: An Introduction for Faculty and Academic Administrators, 2nd ed., NACUBO, 1994.

A Cost Accounting Handbook for Colleges and Universities. NACUBO, 1983.

"How to Develop an Effective Budget Process," by Kent John Chabotar in *Roles and Responsibilities of the Chief Financial Officer*, edited by Lucie Lapovsky and Mary McKeown-Moak. Jossey Bass, 1999.

Implementing Zero-Based Budgeting at Stanford University, by Karen Bennett, Larry Owen, and Timothy Warner. NACUBO, 1983.

"The Importance of Budgeting," by M.J. Gross, M. Warshauer, and R.F. Larkin, in *Financial and Accounting Guide for Not-for-Profit Organizations.* John Wiley & Sons, 1991.

"Planning and Budgeting," by R.E Herzlinger and D. Nitterhouse, in *Financial Accounting and Managerial Control for Nonprofit Organizations.* South-Western Publishers, 1994.

SETTING TUITION

Deciding how much to charge for the institution's "product" ultimately is the board's responsibility. Few other board decisions affect so many, are watched so closely, and are so vulnerable to comment and criticism. Over time, few other decisions so cumulatively and profoundly shape the institution. Setting tuition and fees goes right to the heart of the institution's reputation for affordability and accessibility.

Setting tuition can be easy or complicated. It's an easy task when the board adopts a simple formula, such as: "Tuition will increase at the rate of growth in the Consumer Price Index (CPI) plus 1 percent" and then monitors its growth in relation to the tuition rates of peer institutions.

This pricing policy becomes complicated, however, when the board really examines its implications and consequences. For example: Does our pricing help or hurt in attracting the type of students we want to enroll? How many students actually pay the full published price? Do we use financial aid strategically to recruit a freshman class with certain characteristics, or do we use it to attract the greatest number of students? Is our price competitive? What is our net tuition after financial aid? How dependent are we on tuition revenue?

This chapter is intended to help trustees understand the relationships among tuition, financial aid, and enrollment. It suggests questions trustees can ask of administrators, and recommends what data are needed to make informed decisions.

The Public Debate. The increase in the cost of a college degree has become one of the most heated social and political issues of the day. Countless editorials and feature articles lament the escalating cost of an undergraduate education. The perception of many is that tuition is too high and students are not receiving fair value in return. Higher education is depicted as profligate and aloof.

In 1998, Congress responded to this

growing hostility by establishing the National Commission on the Cost of Higher Education, an independent board chaired by William E. Troutt, then president of Belmont University in Nashville, Tenn. The commission's report, "Straight Talk about College Costs and Prices," acknowledged the concerns of taxpayers and tuition-paying adults about price and affordability:

> Public anxiety about college prices has risen along with increases in tuition. It is now on the order of anxiety about how to pay for health care or housing, or cover the expenses of taking care of an elderly relative. Financing a college education is a serious and troublesome matter to the American public...What concerns this commission is the possibility that continued inattention to issues of cost and price threaten to create a gulf of ill will between institutions of higher education and the public they serve. We believe that such a development would be dangerous to higher education and the larger society.

Trustees of independent institutions are responsible for being stewards of the public trust *and* for ensuring their institutions have sufficient resources to carry out their missions. Balancing these competing needs is difficult, of course. It requires an informed and strategic pricing strategy. It requires trustees to understand how price influences the institution's attractiveness to students and the types of students the institution seeks to enroll. In the end, setting tuition is a complicated calculus that must account for philosophical and financial variables.

Tuition Basics. The published price of a college or university education usually is divided into three distinct parts:

• *Tuition and Fees.* At most private institutions, tuition covers students' costs to enroll in four or five courses per semester or quarter. Some colleges charge by the course or course hour, especially those that have a high percentage of part-time students. Mandatory fees vary among institutions and cover a wide range of activities— student-health charges, use of athletic facilities, student activities, laboratory use, and so on.

• *Room and Board.* Colleges charge residential students a separate fee for housing. Generally, these fees are billed by semester or quarter and include utilities, except telephone. Few institutions charge extra for Internet access. Room rates sometimes depend on whether the room is a single, double, or part of a suite. Students typically choose from a variety of meal plans.

• *Books, Travel, Living Expenses.* Tuition, fees, room, and board constitute the institution's "comprehensive fee." To determine the total cost of attendance, colleges also add in books, travel, and everyday living expenses. Thus, when students ask about the cost of attending a private institution, for example, they may receive an annual "student

Tuition		$20,000
Fees		$2,000
	Subtotal	*$22,000*
Room		$3,400
Board		$3,300
	Subtotal	*$6,700*
Subtotal, Comprehensive fee		$28,700
Books, miscellaneous expenses		$2,000
Total student expense budget		**$30,700**

expense" budget that looks something like the accounting above.

The total student expense budget is a critical number in calculating the amount of financial aid for which a student might qualify at those institutions that award financial aid on a need basis.

How Tuitions Are Set. The tuition-setting processes at private institutions tend to follow similar paths. First, finance officers compare the current tuition at their institution with that at peer institutions. Comparisons are made on current and historical data, not on what institutions plan to do. (Some years back, college administrators freely exchanged information about planned tuition increases, but the U.S. Department of Justice determined that such practices constituted price fixing and were illegal.)

Next, officials analyze the rate of increase in the Consumer Price Index (tuition increases often are reported by the media in relation to the CPI). Consequently, many institutions index

their increases to the CPI. Although quite common, this practice is not financially sound because it does not reflect the market value of goods and services colleges use.

A better index is the Higher Education Price Index (HEPI), though few members of the media and the general public generally are familiar with it. Faculty and staff compensation constitute 75 percent of the HEPI. Compensation typically accounts for 60 percent to 80 percent of the cost of running education institutions. Annual increases in the HEPI have been greater than those in the CPI since the early 1980s. Before that, the CPI grew faster than the HEPI because faculty and staff salaries did not keep pace with inflation.

Another key statistic used as a benchmark for setting tuition is the growth in disposable income, which is a good proxy for the amount of money families have for expenses such as higher education. If tuition increases faster than the disposable income available to the population from which the college attracts students, the college eventually will price itself out of the market. A simple graph showing the real growth (after inflation) in tuition and the real growth in disposable income over a ten-year period can be extremely useful for assessing tuition trends at your institution.

Bottom Up Versus Top Down. At the risk of oversimplifying the long and arduous process of building an annual operating budget, the amount of revenue needed to balance a budget can influence the size of the tuition increase. This "bottom-up approach" involves developing the expense budget first and then examining revenue. After expenses are established, the sources of revenues are estimated—gifts, endowment support, sponsored research, and other

Institutions simply cannot afford to set tuition below a level the applicant pool is able and willing to pay.

miscellaneous income. The remaining item is tuition, the largest revenue contributor in private institutions, which then closes the gap.

This process falsely assumes that price will not affect enrollment. Few institutions build their operating budgets using the bottom-up approach because tuition increases are affected by many factors other than the size of potential budget deficits. Thus, a top-down approach helps prevent the practice of backing into tuition increases and encourages a slower rate of tuition growth.

Pricing Strategies. Colleges employ a variety of pricing strategies. One strategy that dominated higher education for several years is called the "high-tuition, high-aid" approach. This strategy assumes that parents and students equate price with quality. It has two significant drawbacks.

First, college leaders no longer can justify tuition increases that greatly exceed the rate of inflation. Second, many colleges have difficulty finding enough academically capable students who are able to pay high tuition. This condition leads to underenrollment and results in a greater percentage of students who require financial aid.

"Low-tuition, low-aid," obviously, is the opposite strategy. It is based on the assumption that "best bargain" is more attractive to students than "highest quality." Which strategy produces the highest net revenue? The answer is elusive.

The most common approach to setting tuition is to remain competitive within your peer group. Some college leaders believe their institution can be the price leader of their peer group; others pride themselves on being the least expensive; most try to fall in the middle third. This strategy explains, in part, why tuition charges among peer institutions are relatively similar.

Regardless of the specific strategy used by an institution, an often-heard comment at tuition-setting time is not to "leave money on the table." Such a comment may sound cynical to those unfamiliar with the difficulty of balancing an operating budget. However, academic institutions simply cannot afford to set tuition below a level the applicant pool is able and willing to pay. The needs are simply too great.

More Art Than Science. Here's how the process works. The administration recommends a tuition increase to the board after a lengthy process that includes considering how the institution compares with peer institutions, the competitive position to which the institution aspires, budget pressures, the rate of inflation, and the estimated amount of disposable income available to tuition-paying families. In the final analysis, a tuition hike is a business judgment—as much art as science. Following a tuition announcement, finance officers hope they and the board made the right decision, but only final enrollments tell the story.

Setting tuition is a crucial decision, one dependent on many variables. The reality is that only a fraction of students pay the published price. Nevertheless, the published price is important because it sets the boundaries for tuition discounting and determines the general subsidy all students receive.

Financial Aid and Tuition Discounting. The competition for high-ability students is fierce. In 2000, 1.26 million students took the SAT exam. Only 21 percent scored 1,200 or greater. (Forty-six percent scored less than 1,000.) If high-scoring students were divided equally among the nation's 3,200 traditional colleges and universities, each institution would enroll fewer than a hundred high-ability students in its freshman class. It doesn't work that way, of course.

All institutions want to attract gifted students. High-quality students attract other high-quality students and help the college recruit outstanding faculty.

Professor Henry Hansmann of the Yale Law School summarized the importance of attracting high-quality students in a 1999 paper titled "Higher Education as an Associative Good," in *Forum Futures*.

When choosing among undergraduate colleges, for example, a student is interested not just, or even primarily, in the colleges' faculty, curriculum, and facilities, but also in the intellectual aptitude, previous accomplishments, sociability, athletic prowess, wealth, and family connections of the colleges' other students. The reason is obvious: These and other attributes of a student's classmates have a strong influence on the quality of the student's educational and social experience, the relationships (including marriage) that the student will have in later life, and the student's personal and professional reputation.

All college presidents and trustees want to improve the academic reputation of their institutions. The key to doing so lies in the quality of students and faculty, of course, and improving the ranking and prestige of an institution is a never-ending process. Because there are too few highly able students to go around, many institutions use pricing policies and financial-aid awards strategically to attract their share of such students. It is tricky work.

Financial Aid. Administering financial aid is anything but simple or straightforward. The first decision financial-aid administrators must make with their boards is how much financial aid the institution can afford. Only a handful of institutions can afford to sustain totally need-blind admissions policies. Such policies allow institutions to admit students without regard to their ability to pay by providing all the scholarship and grant money required to ensure that all accepted students are able to attend.

Harvard University's then-President Neil Rudenstine spoke about need-blind admissions policies when he testified before the National Commission on the Cost of Higher Education:

> We have made it a cardinal principle that students should be considered for admissions without regard to their financial need. We want our doors to be open to the most able and promising students—rich, poor, or in between. That is only half the principle. The other half—one that converts ideal into reality—is that students who are admitted, and who choose to come to Harvard, are provided with a package of financial aid that is sufficient to enable them to attend.

A handful of institutions, Harvard among them, are blessed with large endowments and affluent, high-quality applicants and have adopted a need-blind policy. Each year brings a roll of the dice to determine how much financial aid their budgets require.

The vast majority of colleges and universities operate in a financial reality different from Harvard's. Unlike Harvard, they are forced by circumstances to limit the financial aid they can offer promising-but-needy students. They simply do not have the financial underpinnings that permit need-blind policies. For institutions with small endowments, financial officers must calculate annually the amount of financial aid they can afford.

This is deadly serious business, and the stakes are high. The pressure to increase financial aid is unrelenting because "buying" quality and diversity in the student mix requires money.

Financial aid typically is one of the fastest growing areas of academic budgets. Given the need to restrict financial-aid funds, colleges must decide how best to spend these limited resources. A variety of approaches exist. But an institution first must resolve a fundamental policy question: Should financial-aid awards be based on student need? If the answer is Yes, then the second question follows: How will need be determined?

An institution may take another approach and decide that a better use of its limited financial-aid budget is to award scholarships based on academic merit rather than need. This strategy can be useful in attracting a critical mass of high-ability students, but often at the expense of underenrolling an entering class.

The Federal Method. If a college or university receives federal funds for financial aid, it operates with some constraints on how it calculates need. But the law is somewhat flexible and provides room for professional judgment. Most colleges and universities use the federal method to compute students' need for financial aid.

The federal method is based on a family's adjusted gross income and the number of family members who are college students. It is fairly generous, but it does not account for the equity a family may have in other assets. Many institutions adjust the federal method to add home equity and savings to the adjusted gross income.

Finance and financial-aid officers must be experts on tax issues, understand the intricacies of a balance sheet, and know how to determine the worth of a small business—all while dealing with parents who may disagree about

what they can or cannot afford. A financial-aid officer must exercise a great deal of judgment to determine the level of aid to which a student is entitled. Invariably, that judgment is subject to criticism.

Once the level of need is determined, the officer compiles a financial-aid package, which includes a component called "student self-help"—summer and academic-year employment and federally funded student loans. Students are expected to earn a proscribed amount over the summer and during the academic year. While on campus, they may be employed for 20 hours a week or more in a federally funded work-study program, which is designed to provide employment opportunities for students receiving financial aid. Students also may choose to work in a

EXAMPLE OF AN AID PACKAGE		EXAMPLE OF AID PACKAGE WITH OUTSIDE SCHOLARSHIP	
Cost of Attendance	$33,654	Cost of Attendance	$33,654
Parent Contribution	-$11,000	Parent Contribution	-$11,000
Student Contribution	-$ 1,750	Student Contribution	-$ 1,750
($1,600 from summer earnings, $150 from savings)		($1,600 from summer earnings, $150 from savings)	
Financial-Aid Eligibility	$20,904	Financial-Aid Eligibility	$20,904
Financial Aid:		Financial Aid:	
Merit Scholarship	$ 0	Merit Scholarship	$ 3,000
Stafford Loan	$ 2,625	Stafford Loan	$ 0
Work-Study	$ 2,000	Work-Study	$1,625
College Grant	$16,279	College Grant	$16,279
Total Aid	$20,904	Total Aid	$20,904

regular campus job, such as food service. The amount students are required to earn as part of their financial-aid "package" increases each school year. A senior usually is expected to earn more than a freshman.

A typical financial-aid package has three parts: loan, work, and scholarship (or grant). (See the chart on page 35.)

Limiting Financial Aid. Institutions can have a need-blind admissions policy but still not meet every student's financial need. In fact, this is quite common. The practice is called the "need aware" policy. A number of options exist for awarding financial aid on a "need aware" basis:

• *Deny/Deny*. In this situation, a student who is aid-eligible but not considered exceptional enough to receive a financial-aid award is denied admission. Institutional officials reason that such students will continue requesting financial aid, or they will have to assume such significant financial burdens that their educational experience will be compromised.

• *Admit/Deny*. In this situation, a marginally qualified student who needs financial aid is accepted but denied financial aid. If the student can figure out a way to pay the tuition, he or she will enroll.

• *Admit/Gap*. This practice admits a qualified student but meets only a portion (or gap) of his or her financial aid. It's up to the student or parent to fund the difference.

• *Differential Packaging*. In these cases, financial-aid officers award students with similar financial-aid needs different aid packages. The more attractive the student, the better the package. For example, one student may receive a larger scholarship and a lesser loan burden, while another receives work-study and a loan.

• *Match Competing Offers*. Many students and parents try to leverage a higher financial-aid package from one college to persuade another college to make a better offer. If the student is highly desirable, the higher award might be matched.

• *Merit Awards*. This is an extreme form of differential packaging. The most desired students receive scholarships even though they may be ineligible for aid. College officials use this strategy to enroll a greater number of high-ability students at the expense of lower ability or needy students.

• *Need-Aware Second Review*. Students who are placed on waiting lists subsequently are admitted based on their ability to pay. Aid-eligible students ordinarily are not considered in the second review.

• *Modify the Methodology for Calculating Need*. The method for calculating need can be changed to make it more flexible. For example, an institution that includes home equity as an asset for student-aid purposes might eliminate it or limit it after a certain threshold is met. The amount of need a student would qualify for can be increased or decreased by changing the methodology.

In the best of all worlds, financial aid

would not be limited, and awarding it would be a simple process. Students who need financial aid would receive it. But most colleges and universities function with limited resources. Their challenge is to use a limited financial-aid budget strategically to leverage it. To that end, it helps to understand the concept of the "demand curve" to meet enrollment targets and ultimately shape an incoming class.

The Demand Curve. A demand curve is best explained by using the analogy of airline-ticket prices. On any flight from Boston to Seattle, passengers may pay different prices for the same kind of seat on the same flight. For those traveling on business, the ticket price may be irrelevant. For tourists and others traveling for pleasure, however, a special price may tip the scale in favor of buying the ticket. The airline wants to fill seats, so it will discount the price to attract enough customers to make the flight to Seattle profitable.

Similarly, colleges want full enrollment. They don't want empty beds and/or classrooms. The difference: Airlines don't particularly care about who are their customers, but colleges do. Colleges want to fill their dorms and classrooms with the most academically capable and well-rounded students they can attract. This is where the analogy breaks down.

To maximize the return on financial-aid grants, finance officers would like to know each student's position on the demand curve. Armed with such knowl-

The leveling off of net tuition, or its actual decline in some cases, is a serious issue.

edge, they would be able to award financial aid perfectly—just enough to enable the student to enroll and not a penny extra that could be used to help another student enroll. While this perfection is nearly impossible to achieve, consulting firms with sophisticated technical skills have emerged to help institutions assess their demand curves.

Finance and financial-aid officers must make these judgments routinely when they deviate from using a consistent methodology to award financial aid. This condition is prompted by "fax wars," which occur after colleges have mailed acceptance letters and have communicated financial-aid awards to students. If a student receives a higher financial-aid offer from a competing institution, he or she often will fax that offer to an institution offering less. Then negotiations begin. Institutional officers must make judgments on the spot, balancing how much the college wants the student and to what degree additional financial-aid might persuade the student to enroll. In other words, where is that particular student on the demand curve? It is a very intense time for all involved.

Tuition Discounting. Trustees must consider two key questions regarding tuition and student subsidies: What is the right level of financial aid? What is the relevance of the published price? In other words: What is our student discount rate?

Not long ago, it was assumed that all students would pay full tuition, and the financial-aid budget (from restricted and unrestricted sources) was calculated as an operating expense. In 1996, the American Institute of Certified Public Accountants (AICPA) audit and

In reality, all students receive a subsidy even when they pay full tuition.

accounting guide was revised to include a new guideline for the display of tuition discounting at private institutions. The AICPA concluded that financial aid was a *discount* from the published price and not an operating expense. Under the new guidelines, private higher education institutions now are required to discount tuition revenue by the amount of institutionally funded financial aid. (The Government Accounting Standards Board imposes a similar requirement on public institutions. This requirement takes effect for fiscal years starting after June 15, 2001.) Thus, financial aid no longer is treated as an expense on the debit side of the ledger. Statements of Activities (which all private institutions must report) now display gross and net tuition. For example, a typical statement of activities (see page 8) shows net tuition and then subtracts university-sponsored financial

aid and donor-sponsored financial aid to derive a net financial figure.

Highly selective colleges and universities argue that financial aid is an expense and not a discount because they can fill their classes with high-ability, full-tuition-paying students if they so choose. These institutions do not award financial aid to increase overall revenue; rather, they do so to attract specific kinds of students. Therefore, argue highly selective institutions, financial aid is a legitimate educational expense.

Only a handful of colleges and universities fall into this category, however. Most private colleges rely on financial aid to meet enrollment targets. For these colleges, awarding financial aid increases revenues. Given the high fixed costs of running a college, the marginal cost of enrolling an additional student is relatively low. If students are added above the enrollment target, however, the marginal cost can be significant because additional faculty and space may be required to serve the student. In the world of enrollment management, most institutions use financial aid to meet enrollment targets and improve the quality and diversity of their student body.

For most of higher education, net tuition is increasing at a slower rate than gross tuition. The reason: Financial-aid costs (the tuition discount) increase faster than the published price of tuition. The published price tends to increase at a fairly predictable rate, while net tuition increases somewhat erratically. The leveling off of net tuition, or its actual decline in some cases, is a serious issue for many colleges.

Net tuition is what you take to the bank. A college must expect to accumulate a specific amount of net tuition to balance the budget. Officials should monitor the relationships among the published tuition price, financial aid, net tuition, and the true cost to educate a student. Trustees should ensure that the administration can answer two basic questions: (1) What is the effect of the published tuition price on financial aid and net tuition revenues? (2) To what extent must the published price increase to yield a targeted level of net tuition? Trustees also should keep their eyes on the institution's "total discount rate." It is important to be concerned about trend lines.

Answering these questions requires a fairly complicated tuition-discounting model. However, finance officers also should be able to construct a simple graph displaying the relationship between gross and net tuition to help trustees monitor trends in this crucial area. An example appears below.

Price, Cost, and Subsidy. It is important for trustees and the general public to understand the differences among price, cost, and general subsidy. Gordon O. Winston, an economist at Williams College and a principal in the Williams Project on the Economics of Higher Education, has written extensively on this subject. He suggests that all students actually receive some form of subsidy and that tuition covers only a fraction of the true cost to educate a student. *In reality, all students receive a subsidy even when they pay full tuition.*

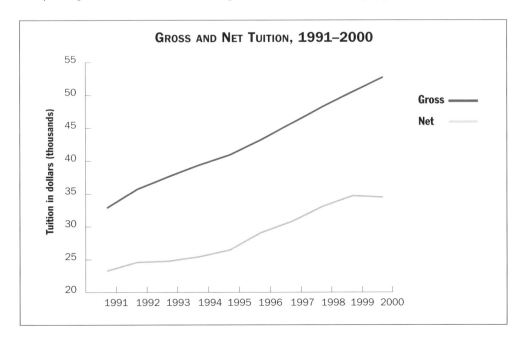

This makes higher education an extraordinary value, Winston argues in a paper delivered to the National Commission on the Cost of Higher Education, "College Costs: Subsidies, Intuition, and Policy":

> The most fundamental anomaly in the economics of higher education is the fact that virtually all U.S. colleges and universities sell their primary product—education—at a price that is far less than the average cost of production. The subsidy that goes to nearly every college student in the country is neither temporary, nor small, nor granted only by government institutions: [S]tudent subsidies are a permanent feature of the economics of higher education; they represent a large part of total costs; and they are only slightly smaller in private than in public institutions. In total, student subsidies exceeded $82 billion in 1995.

Knowing the size of an institution's subsidy is important, but it is not an easy calculation. Most institutions have cross-subsidies, and this makes the calculation more complicated. A simple way to calculate an institution's subsidy is to divide the cost of education (total expense) by the number of students. This yields the "average cost per student." Subtracting the published price (tuition) from the average cost produces the subsidy. The simple formula is "subsidy equals cost minus price."

The problem with this approach is

that it does not address what economists call the "joint products" problem. For many institutions, the costs incurred simultaneously support several different institutional goals and products, which can include undergraduate and graduate education, student and faculty research,

Allowing tuition to increase faster than most applicants' ability to pay is self-defeating.

and public service. The classic example of a cost that cannot be easily divided up is the library. A book may be used by an undergraduate, a graduate student, a researcher, and so on. For institutions with a mission broader than undergraduate teaching, allocating library costs to determine the true cost of educating an undergraduate takes some work.

In 1998, NACUBO assembled a group of finance officers from all sectors of higher education in the hope that a common methodology could be fashioned to determine the size of subsidy for a vast array of higher education institutions. The goal was to develop a methodology that would be accurate enough to be useful and simple enough to be calculated and widely understood. This proved to be a difficult undertaking, and in 2001 the group was still working to refine a methodology that would be relevant for all sectors of higher education.

The reason this issue is so important

is that the public does not appreciate what it costs to educate a student. And there is a debate on whether a high subsidy should be a matter of pride or embarrassment. For a student, a high subsidy surely is a good thing— that is, receiving a $30,000 education (cost) for $15,000 (price). For an institution, it could be viewed as poor fiscal management.

Trustees should know the size of the subsidy, how it changes over time, the relationship between subsidy and tuition, and the true cost to educate a student. Regardless of an institution's specific data about costs, trustees must keep in mind that setting tuition requires tradeoffs among quality, price, subsidy, and mission.

The Board's Responsibility. What information do trustees need to make informed decisions about tuition? Clearly, they must rely on the financial-aid officer and the chief financial officer to recommend a pricing strategy. In addition, they must be able to answer the following questions:

• How does tuition at our institution compare with tuition at peer institutions?

• How does the rate of tuition growth compare with the Consumer Price Index and the likely disposable income of our applicant pool?

• What is the difference between gross tuition and net tuition?

• What are the trends for price, cost, and subsidy for the last five years?

• What is the percentage of students who receive financial aid?

• What is the average financial-aid grant?

• What methods do we use to award and control financial aid?

• How does the academic performance of our full-financial-aid students compare with that of full-paying students?

• What are the loan and work expectations of financial-aid students?

Transparency and Honesty. Advocates and critics alike of higher education increasingly demand that colleges and universities reveal more about price, cost, and subsidy so that students and parents can make informed decisions. The National Commission on the Cost of Higher Education found that "College finances are far too opaque. Higher education has a major responsibility to make its cost and price structures much more 'transparent'… and easily understandable to the public and its representatives." Trustees should make certain their institutions provide the clearest and most accurate information about cost structure to all applicants.

In their book, *The Student Aid Game*, Michael S. McPherson, president of Macalester College, and Morton Owen Schapiro, president of Williams College, plead with institutions to be honest in their financial-aid policies:

There is at least one principle we believe to be of great importance: the principle of honesty and openness in explaining the policies the institution pursues. Such a policy is valuable for several reasons. First, it is essential to allowing students to make reasonable choices among alternatives. If, in fact, applicants will not be admitted from the waiting list if they applied for financial aid, they need to know that policy to decide whether to withdraw their aid application. Second, open policies can be discussed and weighed by the community that has a stake in them—trustees, faculty, students, and alumni. Because colleges are not simply businesses but rather institutions held in trust, it is especially important that their policies be capable of surviving examination by their constituencies.

It bears repeating that trustees should understand the demand curve. Every institution admits applicants who chose not to attend. Where did they enroll instead? If they enrolled in less expensive institutions, price may have been a deciding factor. If they enrolled in equally expensive institutions, then perceived quality may be an issue.

Regardless of an institution's standing compared with its peers, it will find that allowing tuition to increase faster than most applicants' ability to pay is self-defeating. Either the institution will have to limit the size of the applicant pool and be less selective, or it will have to increase its financial-aid budget to make tuition affordable.

Establishing the policies that determine tuition and the amount of subsidy each student will receive ultimately is the board's responsibility. Setting tuition is central to nearly every aspect of an institution, including its mission, the size and quality of the student body and faculty, perceived quality, affordability, and accessibility. This chapter has argued that tuition pricing must be decided relative to many other factors. In the end, it is a judgment call, but its impact over time on the institution's fiscal health and vitality is enormous.

Trustees should become informed about their institution's pricing and discounting policies so they are better able to ask probing questions and gain awareness of the data needed to make these decisions annually.

Recommended Readings

"Are Price Wars Coming to Higher Education?" by Arthur M. Hauptman, in *Trusteeship*. AGB, September/October 1994.

"Costing and Pricing," by Hans Jenny, and "Decision Processes" by John Dunn, from *College and University Business Administration*, 5th ed. NACUBO, 1992.

"Do Private Colleges Make Big Profits?" by Gordon O. Winston, *Forum Futures*, NACUBO, 1998.

"Ensuring Access, Strengthening Institutions," by Stephen Lewis, in *College Board Review*, Spring 1995.

"Higher Education as an Associative Good," by Henry Hansmann, *Forum Futures*. NACUBO, 1999.

"In Tuition Matters: The Bottom Line Counts," by Terry W. Hartle, in *Trusteeship*. AGB, July/August 1996.

Keeping College Affordable, by Michael S. McPherson and Morton Owen Schapiro, Brookings Institution, 1991.

"A New Equation for Tuition and Aid Policies," by Arthur Hauptman. *AGB Priorities*, Number 8, Spring 1997.

"Positioning for Competition," by Lucie Lapovsky and Loren Loomis Hubbell, in *Business Officer*. NACUBO, March 2000.

"Private College Pricing: Are Current Polices Sustainable?" by David W. Breneman, Lucie Lapovsky, and Daniel Myers. Forum for the Future of Higher Education, September 1998.

"Straight Talk about College Costs and Prices." The Report of the National Commission on the Cost of Higher Education. American Council on Education and Oryx Press, 1998.

The Student Aid Game, Michael S. McPherson and Morton Owen Schapiro. Princeton University Press, 1998.

Tuition Discounting, by Loren Loomis Hubbell, NACUBO, 1992.

"Why Does College Cost So Much?" AGB, 2001.

CHAPTER 4

MANAGING THE ENDOWMENT

To understand the governing board's financial responsibility to manage the endowment, it is important to comprehend the concept of stewardship of financial assets. Effective endowment stewardship obligates the board not only to invest endowment funds with care, skill, and prudence, but also to set prudent spending policies that support and benefit current and future students equally.

Endowment oversight is time consuming and requires specific expertise. It involves decisions about how and where to invest, how to match an institution's risk tolerance with expected return, and how to explain to benefactors the endowment's significance to the institution.

This chapter is not a treatise on endowment investing. Rather, it reviews basic responsibilities of investment committees, pays particular attention to the composition of investment committees,

and describes the duties of its members. It explores risk-tolerance concepts, endowment-spending policy, and asset-allocation and investment policy guidelines. The chapter will not make a trustee a professional money manager. It is intended to help trustees understand the basic responsibilities, issues, and vocabulary of investment committees. It certainly is relevant to the investment committees of foundations affiliated with public colleges or universities and to virtually all private institutions—but less so to public institution governing boards that do not oversee endowments.

The Trustee's Responsibilities. Endowments can be vital sources of revenue. Because the size of an institution's endowment often is viewed as a proxy for its financial strength and success, preserving it can become an end in itself. This preoccupation is understandable, but boards should not spend disproportionate amounts of time attempting to increase the endowment at the expense of addressing other critical issues.

Skillful endowment management can improve the long-term wealth of institutions significantly. Endowments grow through gifts, investments, and by transfers of budget surpluses. An endowment's growth often is viewed as an important measure of how well the board carries out its fiduciary responsibilities. Certainly they count in the ranking schemes of various popular magazines.

Trustees often have experience in business or finance, and some trustees have more investment expertise than the financial staff of their college or university. When such trustees are assigned to a board's investment committee, they can make important contributions. The most celebrated case of a trustee's investment expertise benefiting a college occurred at Grinnell College in Iowa. Grinnell's endowment under the guidance of Wall Street investment expert Warren Buffet grew enormously in the 1990s, as have the endowments of other institutions fortunate enough to have professional investment advisers as board members. But such instances are unusual, and it generally is not a good idea to entrust judgments to individual trustees. Investing has become increasingly complex, with a mind-boggling array of investment opportunities. Portfolio management is not for investment amateurs.

One of the most important responsibilities of board leadership is to ensure that the investment committee includes the best talent available. Not only must investment committee members possess sophisticated investment backgrounds, but they also must be able to devote sufficient time to be able to monitor investment managers, make asset-allocation decisions, and perform all of the other tasks involved with overseeing a significant financial enterprise. The board must feel comfortable that the committee has the right talent at the table to make informed decisions. Boards can achieve this in several ways:

• Appoint board members who have sophisticated investment knowledge and experience and who are willing to devote a considerable amount of time to the investment committee's work.

• Appoint nontrustees to the investment committee who have the required expertise. These members may be alumni or potential trustees.

• Delegate to a third party the responsibility for endowment management.

• Engage a consulting firm to work regularly with the investment committee. The consulting firm guides the committee, provides expertise, and identifies issues.

Organizing and Staffing the Investment Committee. The size and complexity of the investment portfolio influence how the investment committee is organized and how many professional investment staff members are needed to manage and monitor the endowment.

Investment committee tasks and decisions include understanding how the endowment supports the institution's mission, developing an endowment-spending policy, determining the board's tolerance for risk, developing an asset-allocation strategy and investment

Portfolio management is not for investment amateurs.

guidelines, selecting managers and monitoring their performance, overseeing the issuance of debt, and voting proxies. In addition to endowment-related tasks, investment committees sometimes are asked to oversee investments in employee pension and deferred-giving plans, though the board's finance committee more frequently is the venue for this task.

The investment committee sets asset allocations, performance standards, and investment guidelines. It commonly uses an outside consultant to help identify important asset-allocation issues, recommend portfolio managers, and measure the performance of outside investment managers. External investment managers invest the funds. This enables the institution to maintain a relatively small staff. The vice president for finance and administration (or a senior executive with a similar title) is responsible for implementing the investment committee's decisions and monitoring external investment managers' performance and compliance with investment guidelines.

Institutions with the largest endowments typically create separate management companies to invest funds and maintain alternative portfolios with internal managers for venture capital, real estate, leveraged buyouts, hedge funds, and so forth. One important rea-

son for doing so is to attract skilled investment professionals by paying market salary rates.

The organizational structure that works best for any specific institution will depend on the size of the endowment, the complexity of the investment portfolio, the talent resident on the board, and institutional history. And while organizational structure is important, it is not as important as ensuring that the right talent manages the endowment.

When appointing trustees to the investment committees, perceived or real conflicts of interest must be monitored. Most institutions have strict policies concerning conflicts of interest. Most situations are reviewed on a case-by-case basis, with full disclosure required for any perceived or real conflict. Underperforming investment managers are much more difficult to fire if trustee relationships also are at stake. Most egregious, of course, are situations that allow a trustee or a trustee's relative to gain financially from an institution's investment transaction.

Endowments and Missions. Endowments provide financial underpinnings to institutions and enable them to weather financial vicissitudes, make revenue available to operating budgets, support programs that otherwise might not be funded, issue debt at favorable rates, and provide financial flexibility. Healthy endowments enable colleges and universities to keep pace with changing information technology, pedagogy, and curricular demands. Obviously, institutions fortunate enough to have large endowments have a competitive advantage over those with small endowments.

The degree of flexibility in an endowment is important. Endowments are classified as "permanently restricted," "temporarily restricted," and "unrestricted"—or sometimes "term," "true," or "quasi." Generally, the larger the unrestricted endowment, the greater the financial flexibility. Trustees can designate unrestricted funds for any purpose. Permanently restricted funds also can provide financial flexibility if they support a core function that would have to be supported anyway. For example, restricted endowments created to support faculty salaries relieve the operating budget of salary expenses and allow funds to be used for other purposes. Permanently restricted funds that provide budget relief are considered fungible because they are interchangeable with unrestricted operating funds.

Endowments composed of a high percentage of restricted funds that do not provide budget relief have much less financial flexibility than unrestricted endowments, even when the endowments are similar in size. An endowment's overall size is important, but independent agencies often view the amount of unrestricted funds as the true test of an endowment's financial strength and flexibility.

Institutional leaders must exercise great care in how trust instruments are written so future leaders will not be burdened with maintaining an endowment for a program that no longer supports an institution's mission. That is, agreements that set conditions on the use of restricted endowment gifts should not bind the institution in ways that may contradict the institution's future mission. It is possible—but very difficult—to change the restrictions on an endowed fund if it no longer serves the mission or otherwise contradicts the priorities of the institution.

Board members can help explain to potential donors why restricting an endowment gift with great specificity may not be in the donor's or in the institution's best interests. For instance, a donor who wishes to endow a scholarship for students from a specific high school may discover the scholarship goes unused if there are no students who meet the college's admissions requirements and the scholarship's restrictions.

Endowments as Mutual Funds. Colleges and universities manage their endowments as though they were mutual funds. A mutual fund manager sells shares in the fund's portfolio. As more money is invested in the mutual fund, more shares are issued. When money is withdrawn, shares are sold. All money invested in the mutual fund is pooled together and invested as though it were a single investment. This often is the case with endowments: Permanently restricted, temporarily restricted, and unrestricted funds are invested as though they were one fund. Some institutions choose to invest different endowment classifications separately or differentially.

Just as an investor in a mutual fund owns a part of the whole portfolio, not individual stocks, so it is with the management of the endowment when all funds are pooled. If a donor endows a professorship for $2 million (which is good because it provides budget relief), the endowed professorship fund buys $2 million worth of new shares in the endowment. The shares are valued at the market value on the day they are purchased, just like a mutual fund.

Unitizing the Endowment. The process for controlling the accounting activity of an endowment is called "unitization." Each share of an endowment fund is a unit with a value that changes as the value of the total portfolio changes. Units pay dividends, consisting of yields and appreciation, to the endowed fund that they support. The following example helps explain how unitization works.

Assume the market value of the endowment's total investment pool is $20 million and 100,000 units exist. Each unit would have a current market value of $200 ($20 million divided by 100,000 equals $200). The aforementioned gift of $2 million to support a professorship increases the value of the investment pool by $2 million, for a new total value of $22 million. The donor's gift would buy 10,000 shares in the investment pool ($2 million divided by 200 equals 10,000). Now, the investment pool would have 110,000 outstanding shares valued at $200 apiece. Similarly, if

5,000 units were redeemed to support the operating budget, $1 million would be withdrawn, which is the value of 5,000 units at $200 per unit. The new total market value of the investment pool would be $21 million.

In the case of the endowed professorship, the operating budget would receive approximately $100,000 annually (assuming a 5 percent payout rate) for the professor. If the actual earnings and appreciation on the endowment exceeded the 5 percent rate, the value of the shares would increase accordingly. The following year, the 5 percent payout rate would produce more income because the shares would be worth more. The objective of the payout rate (often called the distribution rate) is to keep up with inflation so the value of the professorship remains constant in perpetuity.

An important point in understanding how unitization works is to remember that an addition or withdrawal from the investment pool only changes the number of units, not the unit value. Only investment performance can change unit values. Many colleges report the performance of their endowment as the increase or decrease in share value. Such reporting resolves the issue of accounting for gifts. Gifts to the endowment can confuse the issue of investment return because new money added to endowments can make them grow even when investments lose money.

The Endowment Spending Rate. Endowment use is as important as preservation and growth. At a minimum, most college financial officers want endowment revenue to be sustainable, predictable, and in line with the operating budget's growth. They view the endowment as a means to an end—to balance the budget and to provide some degree of financial flexibility.

The tension in setting spending rates centers on the needs of current students versus the needs of future students.

Deciding the endowment-spending rate is very important. Typically, two trustee committees set the endowment-spending rate—the investment committee and the finance (or budget) committee. The investment committee is involved because the annual draw on the endowment significantly influences the rate of return needed to support the spending rate. The finance committee is involved because the endowment's contribution to the operating budget can mean the difference between an operating surplus and deficit.

How can a board determine the appropriate spending policy? It first must establish the importance of the endowment to the operating budget and the institution's need to grow the endowment at an acceptable pace. All spending policies share four competing objectives: (1) maximize long-term total

return, (2) maximize annual spending from the endowment, (3) preserve the long-term purchasing power of the fund's principal and its spending distributions, and (4) maximize the stability and predictability of spending distributions. To develop a spending policy, investment committee members should determine which one of the competing objectives is most important to the institution.

The tension in setting spending rates centers on the needs of current students versus the needs of future students and on short-term growth versus long-term growth. Faculty members usually want to spend more on current programs; chief financial officers want to save more for the future or for a rainy day. Trustees often find themselves torn between these competing ideas.

Donors may be surprised to learn their endowed fund will pay out, on average, only 5 percent of the market value. Investment committee members should help explain the importance of maintaining the fund's purchasing power in perpetuity. They also can help communicate investment objectives and spending calculations. Further, they should help benefactors understand how the endowment is invested and with whom the college contracts to invest the endowment funds. Above all, they must assure donors that the institution takes gift stewardship seriously.

Boards typically have two overarching goals for endowments: (1) to preserve the endowment's purchasing power over the long term and (2) to establish a spending rate that allows the unit value to appreciate at the rate of inflation after taking into account the yearly payout. With these goals in mind, a spending rate calculation can be deceptively simple.

If the endowment returned 8.5 percent through yield and appreciation and inflation was 3.5 percent, the spending rate could be as high as 5 percent and still retain the endowment's purchasing power (3.5 percent inflation plus 5 percent spending equals 8.5 percent).

The spending rate also can be expressed in terms of unit value: If the starting value of a unit at the beginning of the year is $100 and the investment performance produces a 8.5 percent return, spending $5 of the new unit value would leave the investment whole with inflation. The unit value going forward would be $103.50. Economists refer to this as preserving the endowment's real (inflation-adjusted) purchasing power.

Setting a spending rate often is more complicated than these examples suggest. In the 1960s, for example, boards commonly spent only income yield—interest, dividends, rents, and royalties—not capital gains. Trustees viewed capital gains on investment transactions as akin to principal and thus restricted them from being spent. This view tended to limit the vehicles in which boards thought they could safely invest. As a result, endowment funds were heavily concentrated in fixed assets.

It should be noted that some states' laws and FASB 116 and 117 might affect the use of endowment gains when donors have not specified it. In most states, gains are considered unrestricted, and an institution may spend them as it sees fit.

The Total-Return Concept. In 1969, the Ford Foundation published *The Law and Lore of Endowment Funds*, which proposed that capital gains on investments could be spent as income. Although the report's timing was unfortunate (the stock market was about to experience a sustained down period), it fundamentally changed how investment committees viewed their responsibilities and made their investment choices.

Committee members grew comfortable with investing more heavily in equities without fear of running afoul of the fiduciary accounting principle that dictated, under the classical trust doctrine, that capital gains of endowment funds only could be added to principal and not be expended. The report argued that endowments were not subject to trust law but rather to the corporate law concept, which viewed the institution as the absolute owner of gifts with the obligation to include gains as income.

Under the corporate law concept, the income beneficiary and remainderman (an interest in an estate that passes to somebody only after a prior interest terminates) usually are the same (the college). Trust law, however, views the income beneficiary and the remainderman as different interests and requires a "fair division" between the income beneficiary and the remainderman (gains traditionally would go to the remainderman).

With the freedom to invest more heavily in equities and to treat capital gains as income that could be distributed, many investment committees adopted the "total return" approach to endowment-fund investment management. This approach emphasized total investment return—traditional yield plus or minus gains and loses. The total-return approach made establishing an appropriate spending policy more complicated because spending then included gains and losses. Because most academic financial officers need reasonably predictable revenue sources, they adopted various smoothing techniques.

Smoothing Techniques. A common approach to calculating a spending rate involves establishing a spending range (say 4.5 percent to 5.5 percent) of the trailing 12-quarter average of the endowment's market value, with the target being 5 percent. By taking the average market value of the endowment for the previous three years, as opposed to using year-end market value, dramatic changes in the endowment's value caused by short-term fluctuations in capital-market returns are minimized.

In this way of smoothing, the denominator would be the average of the trailing 12 quarters (or three years) and the numerator would be the actual amount of funds spent. For example, if the three-year average market value of the endowment were $20 million (the denominator) and spending were

$1 million (the numerator), the spending rate would be 5 percent.

Because the 12-quarter averaging method divides current spending by the average endowment value, this method under favorable market conditions will tend to overstate current spending. This is because a maximum value is used in the numerator and an average value is used in the denominator. Critics of this method say expressing a spending rate where the denominator is an average of three years of endowment values and the numerator is the current spending is misleading. It is the reason budget committees often question whether the spending rate is too low compared with recent growth in the endowment's market value. Some believe that trustees are not spending enough from the endowment for current programs and thus find the 12-quarter averaging method particularly galling.

One potential solution is to average spending and endowment values—to average the denominator and the numerator. Using this technique, the average spending for each quarter is calculated with the average of the endowment's market value for the quarter. The average of the averages then is calculated to produce a spending rate. The difference can be considerable.

Smoothing the spending rate is a highly sensitive issue for faculty and trustees, especially for the budget committee. The method of calculating the spending rate can have significant financial implications. For institutions with especially large endowments, a one-percent increase in spending can be an enormous sum.

Another common approach to smoothing the spending rate is to establish a spending range (4.5 percent to 6 percent of the 12-quarter trailing average) and increase spending annually by a predetermined amount. For example, a college may decide to increase its endowment spending by 2 percent above the inflation rate. If its current spending is $100,000 and inflation is 2 percent, the amount of funds drawn from the endowment for the next fiscal year would be 104 percent of $100,000, or $104,000. If that rate of increase results in spending either above or below the range, the board would make adjustments in the following fiscal year.

Of course, there are many variations on these basic ways of calculating a spending rate. Some institutions use complicated formulas that factor in many variables, but the simple approach that can be easily explained usually is preferable.

Sometimes, market returns are so positive that a board can make special allocations from the endowment for capital purposes, such as improving the physical plant. In these cases, trustees must balance investments in physical assets with investments in financial assets.

Risk Tolerance. Before an investment committee can select or change an asset mix for the investment portfolio, members must have a clear sense of the board's tolerance for risk. Developing a consensus is an important responsibility of the board's leaders and the investment committee. Investing is a matter of risk transfer. When investors purchase stock in a company, they share in the company's fortunes (or misfortunes), and they want to be compensated for their risk taking. Experienced investors assume risks only when they think they will be properly rewarded and when the risk is suited to their comfort level.

The calculated risk the investment committee takes with the endowment depends on how large a role the endowment plays in supporting the operating budget. If the endowment is small and less significant to the financial health of the institution, the board may be fairly relaxed about the level of risk to which the endowment is exposed. If the endowment plays a major role in the financial affairs of the institution, the board may adopt a more conservative investment approach. The investment committee is obligated to educate the full board on risk factors and explain why it recommends a particular strategy for portfolio management.

Boards rarely are concerned about investment risk, except during adverse times in the market. Nonetheless, trustees may focus on the following risks: (1) the endowment losing its purchasing power over time, resulting in the probability of reduced operating support from the endowment (inflation risk); (2) an inability to keep up with competitors (reputation risk); and (3) a misguided assumption of returns of underlying asset classes causing the investments to underperform because they have been invested in the wrong companies or industries (price risk).

Most boards are sophisticated enough to know that the only way to address "inflation risk" is to assume some "price risk" and volatility in returns. Being the steward of an institution's endowment requires risk taking and a long-term perspective.

Developing an Asset-Allocation Strategy. There is no such thing as a perfect asset mix. In fact, there are many ways to meet investment objectives. However, much depends on the level of risk the investment committee is willing to assume and the particular expertise within the committee. Colleges with identical spending policies often have quite different asset mixes.

Asset allocation is an incredibly important determinant of how well an endowment will perform. Numerous studies show that over long periods of time, equities typically produce higher incremental returns than do cash or bonds. Other studies point out that diversification among asset classes and managers is the key to reducing volatility.

Given these facts, a responsible fiduciary will make sure the endowment is hedged against the two most common problems to stock investment—inflation and deflation.

To develop an asset-allocation strategy, an investment committee must establish a return objective. It can choose from these six: (1) achieve a predictable dollar income, (2) protect the principal in dollar terms, (3) maximize current income rather than total return, (4) maximize the principal rather than current income, (5) preserve the real purchasing power of income and principal, and (6) outperform capital markets in which the fund is invested.

Most institutions aim for objectives five and six—the preservation of real purchasing power of income and principal (because this is a fundamental tenet of being in financial equilibrium) and outperforming capital markets (because this grows the endowment and is part of the competitive nature of investing—that is, beating the benchmarks).

The investment committee also must agree on a time horizon within which to achieve its return objectives. Asset allocations are set for the long term, usually five years or more. The ranges within various asset classes should be wide enough to allow for short-term tactical shifts. At a minimum, the time horizon should reflect the period used in calculating the endowment-spending rate. If a three-year average is used, then at least a three-year period should be used to achieve the return objectives.

Liquidity. Part of the process of developing an asset-allocation plan is to consider risk-adjusted returns as they relate to spending requirements. The goal is to maintain enough liquidity to meet projected spending needs without having to liquidate stocks when they are depressed. Most endowments allocate a certain percentage to fixed-income securities. Such investments provide protection against deflation, reduce short-term volatility, preserve capital, and provide liquidity.

The investment committee needs to match the portfolio's liquidity with the known spending requirements. There should be sufficient holdings in cash equivalents and short-maturity bonds to match near-term spending. Balancing the immediate spending needs of the college with the need to grow the endowment over the long term creates a mismatch of financial and investment time horizons. In addition to holding short-maturity bonds, the institution must hold longer maturity, high-quality, and non-callable bonds to protect the portfolio against deflation-induced drops in stock prices and dividends. Investing in fixed-income securities is a balancing act between the need for liquidity and protection against deflation.

Equities as the Dominant Asset Class. Most endowment portfolios include equities—broadly defined as ownership in domestic and foreign companies, publicly and privately held—as the dominant asset class. The reason is obvious. Historically, stocks have out-performed bonds. (Their returns are 36 times greater than high-quality, long-term bonds during the 20th century.) It would be impossible to meet the objective of preserving the purchasing power of principal and income without stocks as the dominant asset class.

Investing in equities can be carried out through passive or active management strategies.

• *Passive Investing.* Passive investing is carried out by investing a portion of the endowment portfolio in an index fund—most often a capitalization-weighted Standard and Poor's (S&P) 500 fund. The S&P 500 fund is composed of stocks of relatively large American companies. This index does not include foreign companies or small-cap companies, which during certain periods have significantly outperformed the S&P 500. Whether an actively managed portfolio will do better than a passive investment depends, of course, on the skill of the investment manager and the amount of risk the investment committee is willing to bear.

Being the steward of an institution's endowment requires risk taking and a long-term perspective.

• *Active management.* Many investment managers believe they can outperform their relevant benchmarks. They believe active management can add value and will justify their fees by superior performance. Some do beat their benchmarks and indices; many do not. Those who beat the benchmark usually do so by assuming more risk.

Investment managers have their own styles or investment philosophies. Just as common equity styles vary among growth, value, opportunism, diversification, or small company, investment managers may prefer to invest globally, restrict investments to domestic stocks, include hedge funds, or otherwise leverage their investments. Most will mix these. Investment managers also may be categorized into focused-growth, moderate-growth, relative-growth, and so on. There is no shortage of views about where the most value can be added. That's what makes portfolio management so interesting and challenging.

The following example shows how one private college reassessed its asset mix at a time when investment returns had fallen persistently below goals. The investment committee asked the vice president for finance to learn about the returns and asset-allocation mix of peer institutions with similar-sized endowments. The idea was to conduct a best-practice study to see what could be learned from endowments with the best total returns over the last ten and 20 years. A financial-services consulting firm was hired to conduct an asset-allocation study, which had three parts:

1. Analyze those endowments with the best total returns over the past ten and 20 years and their asset allocations. Agree on a framework for thinking about asset allocation.

2. Discuss advantages and disadvantages of specific long-term investment strategies, including risk and implementation considerations.

3. Present a well-considered investment strategy to the full board, explaining the risk assumptions used and the rationale for the new asset allocation.

Working with the investment committee, the consultants posed several critical questions:

• If asset allocation (as opposed to manager selection) is the main driver of portfolio returns, what should be the appropriate long-term asset-allocation strategy?

• What functions does the endowment currently (and prospectively) assume in the college's life?

• Given projected spending needs, what rate of return is required to meet spending needs and maintain purchasing power?

• Is this rate of return achievable given the institution's current investment strategy and anticipated rates of return from the capital markets (and inflation level)?

• In attempting to achieve a particular rate of return, what asset-allocation strategies are available to the committee?

• How should the committee define risk? What risks are reasonable, and what risks are intolerable?

• Once a long-term strategy has been developed, how will it be implemented?

The consultants prepared an analysis of the endowments with the best total returns over the past ten-year and 20-year periods. The confidential report discussed asset-allocation decisions as well as investment committee and governance issues. It concluded that the best performing endowments had the following asset-allocation and performance characteristics:

• General high-equity allocations and diversified asset allocation;

• Complex management strategies, especially within the largest peer institutions;

• "Seasoned" (long-term), high-equity, complex portfolios, which not only had superior risk characteristics relative to simple high-equity portfolios, but also outperformed such portfolios during the time period.

As a result of this and other studies, the investment committee concluded that its asset-allocation guidelines of 65 percent equities and 35 percent fixed income were unlikely to achieve the targeted rate of return. Consequently, it increased the portfolios, exposure to equities by significantly increasing the allocation to non-marketable equities, often referred to as alternative investments.

The investment committee arrived at this conclusion after several meetings devoted primarily to discussing the advantages and disadvantages of increasing its position in alternative assets. In the end, committee members believed that the superior returns of domestic stocks and bonds would not continue forever. The consensus was that domestic stocks would revert to their long-term mean averages.

If that occurred, returns obviously would diminish and the portfolio would generate lower returns than would those endowments invested in alternative assets. Committee members also believed that alternative assets could enhance returns without an equal increase in overall portfolio risk. The consultants performed a number of "efficient frontier" analyses that showed how a diversified portfolio with various types of assets—some risky—actually reduced the volatility of the overall portfolio more effectively than a strategy of excluding volatile investments. Diversification works because assets do not rise and fall at exactly the same time or same rate. The offsetting movements, when combined, dampen the swings of total portfolio returns.

The investment committee recognized, of course, that the decision to increase the endowment's exposure to alternative assets was not without risk. Things could go wrong. Among them, domestic stocks could continue to appreciate at a high level of return, alternative-asset managers could perform poorly, and the wrong types of alternative assets could be chosen.

The committee also recognized the inherent disadvantages of investing in alternative assets: (1) They are less liquid than traditional investments; (2) they require a high degree of due diligence; (3) it is difficult to place meaningful valuations on them until they are liquidated; (4) manager fees are higher and more complex; and (5) there is minimal current income—or none at all.

Several years from now, the investment committee and board will know whether they made the best decisions.

Developing Investment Guidelines. Selecting investment managers with diverse investment philosophies and styles provides for a balanced portfolio. Developing investment guidelines ensures that investment managers stay true to their investment philosophies and styles.

For example, guidelines may dictate the amount of cash a manager can hold.

If a manager decides (on his or her own) to hold cash, it can result in too much cash in the overall portfolio—because the investment committee already may have a cash manager with a specific allocation. The same situation can arise if an equity manager opts to invest in bonds without consulting the committee. Investments in bonds might be increased without the committee's approval, and the portfolio then might become unbalanced.

While investment guidelines are important, there is a danger in making them too narrow or restrictive. Often, reasonable guidelines are developed in consultation with external investment managers—and if managers think proposed guidelines may limit returns, the guidelines should be reconsidered. It can be difficult to hold managers accountable for investment results if they are burdened with guidelines that are too constraining.

Investment guidelines also help establish benchmarks against which to judge a manager's performance. Selecting the right benchmark for each manager is important. Doing so establishes goals and greatly influences investment decisions.

A typical benchmark might be to outperform the S&P 500 by 100 basis points or to be in the top quartile of managers with similar investment styles and philosophies. This will force the investment manager to think of performance relative to the benchmark, rather than to an absolute return. Walter M. Cabot, treasurer at Wellesley College,

having observed many external managers over time, believes that overly aggressive benchmarks can inhibit good managers from producing superior returns over the long run. He recently wrote, "Unrelenting pressure to outperform has taken away from the manager the incentive to use judgment when it is needed to protect principal or reduce risks or losses when markets are at dangerous levels."

Monitoring Performance. After making asset-allocation decisions, developing investment guidelines, and selecting external investment managers, the critical job of monitoring performance begins. At this stage, two issues are crucial for investment committees: (1) how often they need reports on the endowment's overall performance and (2) how often they need reports from managers.

Monitoring performance is time consuming. The frequency of reports often depends on the level of staffing in the treasurer's office. External managers should present written reports at least quarterly, and those reports should evaluate performance against investment guidelines and benchmarks. The reports also should note and explain any deviations from investment guidelines. Many investment committees use external consultants to monitor performance or have custodial banks prepare analytical reports on how external managers are doing against benchmarks.

From time to time, the investment committee should request special reports so members can better understand how the portfolio is positioned and its level of risk. For example, a report on stock holdings might show too much overlap if several investment managers hold large blocks of stock in a single corporation. The committee will have questions about the diversity of investment styles, the level of risk associated with having the portfolio concentrated in a few stocks, and so forth. The committee should feel it is getting the right information, in the right quantities, and at the right time to make good decisions.

Rebalancing the Portfolio. The investment committee also must maintain the integrity of the asset allocation by periodically rebalancing the portfolio. It is not unusual for a portfolio to become unbalanced because one asset class overperforms or underperforms over time. Rebalancing the portfolio is critical to enhancing long-term returns; in fact, it can increase returns as much as a well-timed shift in asset-allocation strategies. Rebalancing is difficult, however, because it is counterintuitive. It requires the investment committee to agree to sell "winners" and buy "losers," and it forces the committee to be disciplined in maintaining its asset-allocation strategy and not let the strategy drift.

An investment committee can adopt three basic approaches to rebalancing a portfolio:

• *Calendar rebalancing.* This involves setting a specific date—often at the beginning of the fiscal year—on which the overall portfolio is analyzed in relation to asset allocation. If the portfolio

range for domestic equities is 60 percent, but the equities have grown to 70 percent because of a bull market, 10 percent would be sold and the money would be invested in an asset class that is below the asset-allocation range.

• *Threshold rebalancing.* This involves automatically rebalancing asset class weightings when they exceed normal asset-allocation targets. For instance, if the range for domestic equities is 40 percent to 60 percent (with the target range set at 50 percent), and domestic equities are 55 percent of the total portfolio, domestic stocks would be cut back to 50 percent.

• *Rebalancing to allowed ranges.* This is similar to threshold rebalancing, except that the rebalancing occurs when the asset class exceeds or falls below the asset-allocation range, as opposed to the allocation target. If domestic equities have a range of 40 percent to 60 percent, and domestic equities are 62 percent of the portfolio, 2 percent of the domestic equities would be sold and the proceeds would be reallocated.

An effective rebalancing discipline assumes there are accurate performance data and timely reports. Getting accurate data for the entire portfolio can be more difficult than one might expect.

Using Custodial Banks. An investment committee must choose a bank to hold the endowment's stocks, bonds, other securities, and valuables for safekeeping. This service includes the settlement of all transactions, including purchases, sales, and security loans by transfer of securities or by electronic (book entry) transfer through a central bank. It is known as the "custodial function." Custodial responsibilities also include collecting and crediting income on securities and monitoring corporate actions, such as stock splits, dividends, tenders, and the issuance of warrants.

Colleges with identical spending policies often have quite different asset mixes.

Essentially, a custodial bank is a high-tech bookkeeper—high-tech because the range and complexity of investment options make reporting and reconciliation very difficult.

Custodial banks can make mistakes, even though most transactions are electronic and the banks have sophisticated investment accounting systems. Frequently, reports from the external investment manager and the custodial bank show different rates of return and valuations. These differences must be reconciled. Depending on the structure and complexity of the endowment portfolio, the college's internal staff can spend considerable time checking the monthly statements from the custodial bank. This "nuts and bolts" side of managing an endowment is an important staff responsibility that needs constant attention.

Socially Responsible Investing. Being an investor carries with it the responsi-bility to vote proxies and consider the corporate behavior of the companies in the portfolio. This can be simple or complex, depending on the level of interest among members of the college community in the companies included in the endowment's portfolio.

Any trustee who lived through the divestment issue in the 1980s regarding companies that did business in South Africa knows the importance of taking campus sentiment seriously and of having a well-considered process for dealing with proxy voting and social-responsibility issues. The South Africa divestment issue divided many boards, consumed countless hours for debate and study, and dominated the agenda of many board meetings. More recently, investments in companies that sell tobacco and products made in "sweat shops" of foreign nations have brought renewed student and faculty activism to some campuses.

During "quiet" periods, investment committees often delegate to external managers or custodial banks the respon-sibility for voting proxies. Others create advisory committees to study and consider proxy issues. Having an avenue for student and faculty input is smart policy and can spare the board the angst of protests when issues of investor responsibility heat up.

Deferred-Giving Programs. These pro-grams—under the stewardship of investment committees—involve situa-tions where a college holds a gift in trust and the donor retains an interest in it until his or her death or the death of other named beneficiaries. Deferred gifts come in a variety of forms, including charitable remainder and annuity trusts, pooled-income funds, and charitable gift annuities.

Unlike a donor who contributes to the endowment, a donor who enters into a deferred-gift contract with an institution retains an interest as an income beneficiary. The college's interest is that of the remainderman, and the financial officer seeks to invest the deferred gift so the income requirements are met without eroding the principal.

The college, acting as the trustee, accepts fiduciary responsibility for the assets without financial benefit until the last beneficiary of the gift's income is deceased. By law, stewardship responsibility for deferred gifts is equal to that for overseeing an endowment. In addition to the usual expectations of investing with care, skill, and prudence, the trustee's duty of loyalty extends both to the donor and to the college. The college, as the trustee, is required to balance equitably the needs of both. In many ways, investing deferred gifts is more difficult than investing the endowment because of the need to balance the interests of the income beneficiary and the remainderman.

Investment committees often establish separate investment guidelines for deferred-giving programs. They may create new investment options, such as growth funds, income funds, or high-yield bond funds similar to mutual funds to help market the deferred-giving program. Deferred gifts require significant ongoing administration (which includes preparing income tax reporting forms for donors and distributing payments to donors), so finance officers often engage special custodial banks to invest and administer the program.

Trustees need to establish ground rules for deferred-giving programs. Important policy decisions must be resolved: types of acceptable gifts, the terms of the gifts, and how the assets will be invested, to name a few. Additionally, they must develop policies that spell out minimum allowable gifts and the minimum age and number of beneficiaries.

Investment and development committees also need to make certain that policies governing gift acceptance are established and published for staff and donors alike. The Council for Advancement and Support of Education (CASE) has established guidelines for deferred-gift reporting. Most development offices now report both the market value and the present value of deferred gifts. Written policies can help minimize tensions regarding what is fair for donors and for the institution. However, the chief financial officer usually is authorized to make exceptions to gift-acceptance policies—and situations do arise that require policy exceptions.

A successful deferred-giving program can attract donors who otherwise would not make a significant gift to the endowment—where most deferred-giving proceeds go for most institutions (unless the donor has stipulated otherwise, and the institution agrees). Trustees need to realize the potential of a well-developed deferred-giving program and recognize that a successful program requires careful planning and attention to detail. Investment committees and development committees share responsibility for approving policies that govern deferred-giving programs and for monitoring investment results.

Summary. Managing an endowment is a primary financial responsibility of the board. For institutions with modest endowments, it is not uncommon for the trustee members of the investment committee to have more investment expertise than members of the college's financial staff.

The first responsibility of the board is to make certain the investment committee has a sufficient number of trustees with investment experience to make informed investment decisions. The investment committee's roles are many: determine the amount of risk the institution can assume with its investment policies, develop an asset-allocation strategy, develop performance and investment guidelines, decide between active or passive investing, monitor the performance of external managers, rebalance the portfolio, vote proxies, deal with the social-responsibility issues, and administer a deferred-giving program.

Endowments are managed like mutual funds by a process known as unitization. By unitizing the endowment, all shares have equal value, and the endowment can be invested as a whole.

Trustees must decide on an endowment-spending rate to protect the long-term purchasing power of the endowment while providing an appropriate amount of funds for the operating budget. How well the endowment is managed is frequently used as an indicator of how well the institution is fiscally managed.

Recommended Readings

Board Basics: "Endowment Management" by William T. Spitz. AGB, 1997.

Board Basics: "The Investment Committee," by John H. Biggs. AGB, 1997.

Alpha: The Positive Side of Risk, by Marvin L. Damsma, Jon Lukomnik, Maaten L. Nederlof, and Thomas K. Philips. Investment Press, 1996.

The Developing Law of Endowment Funds: The Law and the Lore Revisited, by William L. Cary and Craig B. Bright. Ford Foundation, 1974.

"Endowment Management," Chapter 10 in *College and University Business Administration*, by David Salem. Vol. 2, Fifth Edition, NACUBO, 1992.

Global Investing: The Professional's Guide to the World Capital Markets, by Roger F. Ibbotson and Gary P. Brinson. McGraw Hill, Inc, 1993.

"Heartfelt and Heady Investments," by Charlie D. Fiskeaux, in *Trusteeship*. AGB, January/February 2001.

Inside the Boardroom: Governance by Directors and Trustees, by William G. Bowen. John Wiley & Sons, 1994.

The Law and the Lore of Endowment Funds, by William L. Cary and Craig B. Bright. Ford Foundation, 1969.

NACUBO Endowment Study (an annual study).

Pioneering Portfolio Management, by David F. Swensen. The Free Press, 2000.

CHAPTER 5

MANAGING
HUMAN RESOURCES

The faculty and staff of a college or university are its greatest assets and are critical to carrying out its mission. Indeed, an institution's reputation rests on the quality of its faculty. However, it is not just faculty but all who work for a college that shape its character.

Managing faculty and staff from a human-resources perspective has many financial ramifications. Colleges are labor-intensive organizations in which 50 percent to 60 percent of the total operating budget (and sometimes more) is devoted to compensation expenses. Faculty compensation alone typically accounts for 30 percent to 50 percent of this amount.

Human-resources management is demanding and complicated. At most academic institutions, three distinct personnel systems exist: one for the faculty, one for the administrative and support staffs, and yet another for those covered under collective-bargaining agreements. The board's most specific fiduciary responsibilities for these three areas concern compensation issues, compliance with applicable laws, and the ability to attract and retain the right people.

Compensation and Benefits. Given the high percentage of salary and benefits in institutional operating budgets, boards must monitor the number of employees and their competitive salary positions; they must know the salary objectives and how those objectives are measured; and they must understand the comparison group.

Selecting the right comparison group is crucial. An institution in a low-cost area should not compare itself to one in a high-cost area—or if it does, it should take cost of living into account and refigure the peer institution's salaries accordingly. Monitoring compensation objectives is crucial. If salaries are too low, the institution will pay a heavy price in the loss of key staff, low morale, or both. If salaries are too high, the campus is likely to have a resource-allocation problem.

It is important to make certain that reward structures are aligned with the institution's objectives.

Academic institutions have few financial options at their disposal to reward outstanding performance. During periods of low inflation, salary pools are necessarily low. If annual salary increases are based solely on merit, there may be only .5 percent difference in raises for outstanding employees and those ranked average. Making creative use of small salary pools is a persistent management challenge.

From the board's perspective, it is important to make certain that the reward structures are aligned with the institution's objectives. If an institution emphasizes a team approach to problem solving, for example, then team problem solving should be a key factor in its performance-management system.

Although board members should not be overly involved in most areas of staff salary and benefits, they do have a significant responsibility related to executive compensation. Providing appropriate levels of compensation for the executive team, particularly the president, is a specific board responsibility. Part of that responsibility is to conduct a formal assessment of the president's performance periodically. (AGB has two excellent resources on these topics: *Presidential Compensation in Higher Education*, by

Robert H. Atwell and Jane V. Wellman, and *Presidential and Board Assessment in Higher Education*, by Richard T. Ingram and William A. Weary.)

Three committees can increase a board's effectiveness in human resources. The first is the compensation committee, a committee that has grown more important with the advent of the "intermediate sanctions" regulations of the Internal Revenue Service. The law requires the board to review the compensation and benefits of the institution's most highly paid employees and determine that the levels are appropriate and reasonably consistent with those of peer institutions. Because previous law limited the IRS to the extreme penalty of withdrawing an institution's non-profit status if salaries and benefits were found to be unreasonable, a less severe penalty—intermediate sanctions—was needed. Under the new law, both highly compensated executives and individual board members can be assessed excise taxes if the IRS finds them culpable. Although this has yet to occur, test cases are likely.

The board's compensation committee must document its meetings and discussions and show evidence that it reviews executive compensation levels against appropriate benchmarks. It is necessary to show some link to performance review as part of the rationale for significant upward adjustments in total compensation. Atwell and Wellman's book discusses this topic in great detail.

A second committee has human-resource responsibilities: the oversight committee devoted to administrative and support personnel management. It is routine for boards to have standing committees that oversee academic affairs and faculty personnel issues, and the board's finance or budget committee often considers the size of the salary-increase pool and benefit changes. But rarely do boards dig deeper into substantive administrative issues, even though the operational side of the campus consumes a large portion of the operating budget and has the largest number of employees. A board oversight committee on staff issues might be helpful. It can request benchmark studies of peer institutions on the size of the staff by functional area, or it might ask for a study on outsourcing strategies. An added benefit: Paying attention to the administrative and support staff sends a powerful message to support staff that the board cares about their welfare, too.

A third committee that may be helpful is an advisory committee that puts specific board members' human-resources experience and influence to work on the college's behalf. Composed of alumni who are senior corporate personnel executives, this advisory committee would help the institution keep current with the latest human-resources practices and expertise. They can explore such matters as cost-benefit ratios of tuition-remission policies and practices and other attractive benefits for faculty and staff.

Management Development and Training. One of the ironies of higher education is that colleges and universities spend so little time and money educating their own employees. Corporations have a much better understanding of the importance of keeping employees well trained and up to date.

Because staff development often is overlooked and underfunded, the board can usefully encourage the administration to address this need. A campus should have financial support and a well-developed program to provide professional development opportunities for staff and the executive team. The most valuable types of professional development include managerial training, regular training in new technologies and software applications, training in an individual's discipline, and training in such business practices as customer service. It also is important that trustees set their own good example. Thus, periodic self-studies of the board's responsibilities, organization, and performance are important every three or four years, preferably with competent and experienced third-party facilitation.

Creating a Diverse Staff. As the students populating our institutions become more diverse, they understandably expect those who are teaching and providing administrative support to reflect their own diversity. Achieving a multicultural workforce requires a strong commitment throughout the organization.

The board can help by monitoring diversity goals and by providing financial support for special initiatives to attract and retain a diverse faculty and staff.

Most campuses have programs to improve the diversity of faculty and staff, but specialized training often is required to create a supportive atmosphere.

The Unionized Campus. A unionized campus presents special challenges because the oversight of faculty who work under a collective-bargaining agreement requires certain knowledge and skills.

The social contract under which unionized faculty operate is based on the collective-bargaining agreement that spells out their conditions of work: teaching loads, promotion processes, salary and benefits, and other economic and workplace issues. On some campuses, the existence of a faculty union is of relatively little consequence; it simply provides an orderly process for setting salaries and benefits. On other campuses, the faculty contract is vitally important and arouses a great deal of tension during contract negotiations.

Trustees should understand two things concerning unionized faculty: (1) the terms and conditions of the collective-bargaining agreement and (2) the issues that are most difficult to resolve at the bargaining table. Trustees with experience working in unionized environments can provide useful advice to deans who may lack similar experience. The board also can provide balanced advice when relationships between union leadership and the administration become strained.

For administrative and support staff, a collective-bargaining agreement dic-tates salary and benefit levels, a classification system, and working conditions. Some of the largest groups on campus—the trades, custodial and food services staff, and police or campus security—are the most likely to organize.

Maintaining positive relations with unionized staff requires supervisors to be skilled in labor relations and grievance handling. Trustees cannot overemphasize the importance of training managers to create a positive work environment. Strikes and work stoppages create great turmoil; the board needs to feel confident that the human-resources office has effective programs for labor relations and dispute resolution.

As is the case with unionized faculty, the board must understand why administrative and support staff join unions, what conditions lead to the organizing effort, and what issues may become problematic. Additionally, through its actions and statements, the board should recognize periodically the important contributions these often-unappreciated workers make to the life of the college. Gestures of recognition and respect make a world of difference.

Unique Issues of Faculty. What do trustees need to know to develop an informed understanding of faculty personnel issues? The information falls into three broad categories:

The "social compact" between an institution and its faculty. To understand the social compact, trustees should probe the following areas:

• To what standards are faculty generally held? What does the institution expect of a faculty member in terms of being available to students for advising, for independent study, for participating in faculty committees, for being a presence on campus?

• What are the expectations for research and scholarship at the institution?

• Is teaching valued as highly as scholarly work? Is there a plan to improve classroom teaching? What are the teaching loads and actual class sizes that most teachers experience?

• How are faculty monitored and mentored at the assistant level, and how are tenured faculty kept current and motivated? How are faculty judged for merit increases?

The academic ethos of the institution. Board members acquire an understanding of the campus ethos, or culture, by talking with the faculty leadership, by dining with varied faculty members, and by talking with students about their classroom experiences. This knowledge makes a tremendous difference in a trustee's effectiveness and enjoyment.

Tenure. To grasp the cultural difference between the worlds of commerce and the academy, a trustee needs to appreciate a professor's life cycle. The road to tenure is filled with pressure because so much is a stake. For the individual, seeking tenure demands years of hard work in teaching, research, and campus service; for the institution, granting tenure to a single individual can mean a $2 million commitment or more.

The tenure process involves a departmental recommendation about whether a candidate has the qualities the department seeks and whether he or she will add value for the next 30 years or more. Typically, tenure decisions are made after the sixth year of teaching. Many institutions have a standing faculty committee that reviews the departments' tenure recommendations. These committees have well-defined procedures and processes.

The standing faculty committee carefully reviews all material and renders an opinion that is sent to the president, who makes a recommendation to the board. Because of the time the faculty committee spends forming its opinion and the careful consideration the president gives to its recommendation, boards rarely refuse to support a tenure recommendation. But boards should not

Tenure standards, tenure review, and the percentage of tenured professors are critically important policy decisions.

simply acquiesce. Through the work of its academic affairs committee, the board must be confident that tenure standards are high, that the tenure-review process has integrity and is being implemented consistently, and that the percentage of faculty who are granted tenure is appropriate. Tenure standards, tenure review, and the percentage of tenured professors are critically important policy decisions that are the board's responsibility.

Special Benefits for Faculty. Faculties have an extraordinary sense of entitlement, due in part to the independence and the sense of commitment to an institution that come with tenure. As part of their oversight responsibilities, trustees should understand the rationale and issues behind four of the most valuable—and expensive—benefits of tenured faculty.

• *Early retirement programs.* With the elimination of mandatory retirement at age 65 came concern that faculty members would not retire until well after they had ceased to be effective teachers and scholars. To encourage them to step down around age 65, many campuses created early retirement incentive programs similar to those found in industry. Special pension supplements may be available to those who retire at a certain age or who participate in a phased retirement program.

Early retirement programs are worthwhile for two reasons. First, they allow for a regular infusion of new faculty, which is critical to keeping a college vital. Second, they usually are cost-effective because salaries of junior faculty are lower than those of long-term faculty members.

• *Sabbaticals.* Over the course of their careers, faculty members may receive four or five sabbaticals; often, these are scheduled automatically every six years

or so. Although sabbaticals are expensive, they are essential to sustaining a professor's intellectual vitality. This also is true for the chief executive and other senior officers, of course.

The critical issues to understand about a sabbatical program include how much it costs, how the campus covers the courses that the professor on sabbatical usually teaches, and how the institution monitors the quality of the research and writing that occur during the sabbatical.

• *On-campus housing.* There are several rationales for providing the faculty with rental housing, subsidized mortgage programs, or both. Residential colleges that encourage easy student-teacher interaction need to have a core group of faculty living close to campus. In addition, faculty housing is a benefit that can be important in faculty recruitment and retention. However, along with faculty housing come a number of complicated policy decisions: determining who is eligible, how long one can stay in faculty housing, who maintains the property, and appropriate rental rates.

• *Tuition support, or discounts, for children of faculty.* Faculty members often do not earn enough to send their children to the college where they teach. Programs can be designed to provide full tuition or half tuition at the home institution or at any accredited institution that agrees to an exchange program.

If a tuition program is limited to faculty, trustees can expect to hear that the benefit is unfair and should be made available to all who work for the college. Trustees should agree to a broader program only after weighing the advantages and disadvantages carefully and understanding the costs thoroughly. Once a benefit is given, it is very difficult to take away.

Changing Times. The world of work is changing everywhere—even in tradition-bound academia. Shifts are evident throughout every campus. A few years ago, every department had at least one secretary. Today, professors do their own typing and make their own appointments. Administrative assistants in academic departments function with higher levels of responsibility, often controlling budgets and providing continuity when department and faculty leadership positions are reassigned to different individuals.

Another change—one influenced strongly by technology—involves how faculty and staff actually carry out their work. More work is accomplished on the Internet, especially via e-mail and the World Wide Web. To keep up, all employees need to be computer literate, which can be a struggle for those who entered the workforce before computers played such an important role.

Then there is the major cultural shift in employee attitudes. The new workforce is more interested in personal and professional growth than in building a career at one institution. Supervisors from other generations often have difficulty understanding this view of loyalty to career as opposed to the institution.

Finally, new research suggests that high-performing organizations should concentrate on improving the activities related to their core mission—and outsource everything else. Higher education has been reluctant to outsource "non-core" functions because of the importance of maintaining a sense of community. The culture of higher education places a high premium on maintaining a "sense of place," the feeling of commitment to the institution's mission, and the comfort of collegial relationships. These qualities make working in academe very special, but regrettably, they may not be sustainable over the long term.

Are external events eroding these wonderful attributes? Definitely. But a certain amount of change simply is inevitable. The board's vital contribution in this area is to help management understand the forces transforming the workplace—inside and outside the academy. The challenge for all will be to adapt to the new work ethic while maintaining and creating anew those special qualities that make working for an academic institution fulfilling and satisfying.

Recommended Readings

"Future of Human Resources," by Fred Foulkes. Chapter 29 in *Tomorrow's HR Management*, edited by David Ulrich, Michael Lasey, & Larry Leke. John Wiley and Sons, 1997.

"Human Resources Management and Employee Relations." Chapter 16 in

College and University Business Administration, 5th ed., by Sigmund Ginsburg. NACUBO, 1992.

"Improving Productivity & Quality in Higher Education," by Aims C. McGuinness, Jr. and Peter T. Ewell. *AGB Priorities*, Fall 1994.

"A New Mandate for Human Resources," by David Ulrich. *Harvard Business Review*, January/February, 1998.

"Performance Appraisals and Pay-For-Performance Plans," by Thomas R. Tudor, Robert Trumble, and Lamont A. Flowers. *Journal of Compensation and Benefits*, November/December 1996.

The Talent Solution: Aligning Strategy and People to Achieve Extraordinary Results, by Edward L. Gubman. McGraw-Hill, 1998.

Taking Charge of Change: Ten Principles for Managing People and Performance, by Douglas K. Smith. Addison-Wesley Publishing Company, 1996.

"The Transformation of the Human Resource Function: Resolving the Tension Between a Traditional Administrative and a New Strategic Role," by Michael Beer. Chapter 8 in *Tomorrow's HR Management*, edited by David Ulrich, Michael Lasey, & Larry Leke. John Wiley and Sons, 1997.

The University: An Owner's Manual, by Henry Rosovsky. W.W.Norton & Company, 1990.

CHAPTER 6

SETTING CAPITAL BUDGETS AND FINANCING DEBT

The board has an important financial responsibility to approve and monitor capital expenses. The capital budget provides an opportunity to set the future strategic direction of the institution while ensuring the institution's physical assets are maintained for future generations of students.

Only a few decades ago, the financial well-being of colleges and universities depended primarily on their human resources. Today, academic institutions are exceedingly capital intensive. This shift helps explain why the cost of education is rising faster than the rate of inflation. On many campuses, the rapid rise in capital expenditures can be attributed to an increase in the use of technology, the need to continually modernize campus facilities, and the cost of maintaining aging infrastructures.

The increased use of information technology in higher education has not

reduced costs. While it has improved the classroom experience and greatly enhanced administrative functions, growing expectations for new technologies and the expense of hiring additional staff to keep computer systems working have added significantly to the cost of educating a student.

Institutions must stay current with advances in information technology or students will go elsewhere. Modern classrooms and laboratories also are essential. Classrooms and laboratories are being retrofitted and upgraded constantly to keep pace with technological change. Doing so is very expensive.

Yet while campuses modernize, the infrastructure that supports new information-technology systems and cutting-edge labs is aging. On most campuses, heating, ventilation, and air-conditioning systems must be upgraded, and every building requires more electrical power and better wiring so computer workstations will operate anywhere students study and administrators work. The pressure to modernize often results in a shift of resources away from maintaining buildings and infrastructure. The result is a growing backlog of deferred maintenance. A 1996 NACUBO and APPA survey identified $26 billion in accumulated deferred maintenance throughout American higher education institutions.

If one of the principles of being in financial equilibrium is maintaining the physical assets over time, how does a board decide how much to spend on capital projects? What policy issues should the board consider in deciding the amount of scarce resources to allocate to maintain and modernize the physical plant?

Capital Project Decisions. Capital decisions are major decisions. Most boards expect to have the final say about where and when new buildings will be added to the campus, who will design and build them, and how the ongoing costs of maintenance will be funded. Decisions about new buildings are easy.

Trustees should be equally concerned about "routine" decisions: maintaining buildings and grounds and ensuring adequate resources for renewal, deferred maintenance, and major renovation. These decisions are difficult.

The board's financial responsibility for capital projects involves reviewing the administration's recommendations for (1) planning new construction, (2) dealing with depreciation and deferred maintenance, and (3) purchasing and maintaining technology and scientific equipment. Further, the board will monitor how capital projects are to be funded.

Buildings should be added to the campus because they are clearly needed, not because funds are available to build them.

In capital budgeting, as in other areas of fiduciary responsibility, the board must ensure that the administration is gathering and analyzing the appropriate facts, that its recommendations are consistent with the institution's mission and board-approved strategic objectives, that costs and benefits are considered, and that everyone fully understands all long-term financial implications for the institution.

Planning New Construction. The decision to construct a building involves multiple board committees. The building and grounds committee and finance committees always are involved; the academic affairs, student life, technology, and development committees sometimes have voices in the decision. The board must make certain the administration has analyzed all the issues that flow from a decision to build and has considered any unintended consequences of the decision. Adding a building will increase the operating budget and fixed costs.

The decision to construct a new facility should be tied to the institution's strategic plan. In making the case for new construction, the emphasis should be on the building's primary and secondary uses and why these activities are important to the institution's mission. One of the most difficult decisions for any board is to turn down a donor's offer to fund the construction of a new building because it is not in the strategic plan or because the donation does not adequately contribute to its maintenance and servicing. Buildings should be added to the campus because they are clearly needed, not because funds are available to build them.

Making this difficult decision—and others that involve new construction—can be a bit easier if the board has a current master plan. A master plan focuses on priorities and links a host of related issues in one planning document. It considers site locations, parking, traffic, deliveries, pedestrian traffic, landscape, and the campus infrastructure.

New construction often is connected to a fund-raising initiative. A master plan can be a powerful fund-raising tool because it demonstrates the depth of thinking that precedes a decision to seek funding for a new building. Unless the proposed building has little fund-raising appeal and must be funded through the issuance of debt, a draw on the endowment, or through a lease-back arrangement (such as a utility building), the board should know in advance the size of the gift required to name the building for a donor. The board also must decide what percentage of the costs should be in hand or pledged before construction can begin. In addition, it must calculate the amount of endow-

ment that will be required for the building's upkeep, staffing, and maintenance.

Dealing With Depreciation and Deferred Maintenance. Budgets are developed from the bottom up, beginning at sub-unit levels—academic, administrative, and student-service departments. The priorities of subunits are for more programs, a larger staff, higher salaries, and more equipment—not depreciation and deferred maintenance. Consequently, boards sometimes must be advocates for unpopular priorities.

How much is enough to spend on depreciation and deferred maintenance? No easy answers exist. Instead, administrators must assure their governing boards that they have a plan for deciding how much of the institution's operating budget should be set aside for preserving physical assets. There are several ways to calculate this budget allocation:

• The *"current replacement value" method,* or the *"back of the envelope" calculation.* To arrive at this calculation, the finance officer calculates the current replacement costs of buildings and other physical assets using published construction costs. Once the finance officer knows the replacement costs for the entire campus, he or she decides what percentage will be reinvested annually to ensure ongoing maintenance, facilities renewal, and space adaptation. The percentage usually ranges from 1.5 percent to 2.5 percent, depending on the condition and age of the facilities. For example, if the replacement value of buildings, infrastructure, roads, and so on is $500 million, then $7.5 million to $12.5 million would be set aside annually, depending on existing conditions.

• *Fund depreciation method*. This method relies on calculations for depreciation and amortization. It is important to realize that this number is calculated on the original cost of assets and improvements.

• *Independent survey method*. The buildings and grounds committee and finance officer might conduct a periodic audit of the physical plant by hiring a consultant or outside construction firm to do an independent assessment. Some trustees support this approach because they view it as part of their due diligence. The typical outcome of an external audit is a list of maintenance needs, together with a list of which needs should be addressed first.

• *The life-cycle calculation method*. Supported by many physical plant directors, this approach involves estimating future renewal and replacement costs for each facility's major subsystems—roofs; plumbing; electrical; and heating, ventilation, and air conditioning. Predicted renewal costs are aggregated by building and time period as a means of projecting total renewal needs into the future.

Often, institutions use a combination of these approaches. But more important than the specific method used to estimate annual capital reinvestment is that some method is being employed at all. Trustees should be concerned if administrators are ad hoc in their approach to funding depreciation and deferred maintenance. The board is not responsible for doing the calculations; rather, trustees must ensure that the administration does them, and so they must understand which calculation methods are used and why.

Technology and Scientific Equipment. How much is enough, and how much is too little? No simple formula exists for estimating technology needs. Computers and software depreciate rapidly, usually within three to five years. (This short time period adds significantly to the amount of depreciation shown in financial statements.)

For the board, policy issues about funding technology center on how and how extensively technology is employed in the academic program and in managing the institution. How the institution is positioned to support technology is equally important. Some colleges are technology "followers"—they want to invest only in proven technology and systems. Others want to be on technology's cutting edge. There are cost implications associated with either position. And while the cost of computing drops every year, the demand for power and memory increases more rapidly.

That technology is transforming all of society is clear. The issues are more profound than simply financial or economic. They center on how the institution is positioning itself for the future—how it teaches, how it prepares for technologically savvy students with high expectations, what it expects of the faculty and staff, and how it keeps up with the rapid pace of change.

Some institutions lease equipment rather than purchase and replace computers every three years. Others buy computers outright and have a replacement policy that varies according to how the equipment is used. Some institutions require students to bring computers with them; others provide computer clusters in dormitories or libraries. Some equip faculty with computers; others require faculty members to purchase their own. All these decisions depend on the institution's policies regarding the importance of computing to its educational mission. Most important for the board is to understand the administration's thinking about technology and to place budget requests for technology in a broader strategic context.

The cost of computing, of course, is much greater than the cost of hardware. Other significant costs include software, training, and staff to keep systems functioning. A number of harsh realities—not all of them financial— arise with each major software decision. Consultants will be needed for extended periods unless major commitments are made to staff education and training.

Most chief financial officers are familiar with the turmoil that follows a decision to purchase financial and administrative software. Staff members may feel like they are doing two jobs at once—their regular job and the tasks associated with installing a new system. The task always is more time consuming and expensive than originally envisioned. And once an institution has invested time and money (particularly for a totally integrated administrative system), it can become hostage to the business plans of the software provider. The provider's schedule of upgrades— which create an enormous amount of work—is beyond the institution's control. There's no turning back. The institution must install the upgrades or run the risk of using software no longer supported by the vendor.

Details like these, however, are the responsibility of the administration, not the board. The board should make sure the administration has done its due diligence and is fully aware of other institutions' similar experiences.

The costs of maintaining well-equipped laboratories and outfitting new ones also are increasing faster than the rate of inflation. It is not uncommon to spend $500,000 or more to equip a new lab or create a new faculty position. Yet such expenses must be accommodated. Students must be exposed to current technologies and instrumentation if they are to be adequately prepared for graduate school or careers. Research contracts and outright grants sometimes are available for purchasing new laboratory equipment or upgrading existing labs, but more often they are not. Some research areas are more attractive to outside sponsors than others; consequently, many colleges use part of the overhead charge to purchase equipment for the areas that normally do not attract outside funding.

Periodically, the finance or budget committee should receive a report on

RATINGS AGENCIES CONSIDER SEVERAL FACTORS IN DETERMINING A BOND RATING

RATIO NAME	CALCULATION METHOD	MEANING AND USE
Selectivity ratio (percentage)	Acceptances divided by applications	Measures demand: What proportion of students who apply are accepted?
Matriculation ratio (percentage)	Acceptances divided by matriculating students	Measures demand: What proportion of students who are accepted come?
Net tuition per FTE students (dollars)	Net tuition and fees revenues divided by total number of FTE students	Measures demand: What are the average tuition and fees actually received on a per-student basis?
Total tuition discount (percentage)	Scholarship and fellowship expense divided by gross tuition and fees revenue	Measures the amount of tuition revenue funded by unrestricted institutional resources and external sources. Often used as a demand measure
II. Operating Results		
Net tuition and fees as a percentage of operating income	Net tuition and fees divided by total operating income	Used as a measure of "tuition dependency"
Operating margin (percentage)	Operating income divided by total operating revenues	Traditional measure of "profitability" in operations
Gift and investment reliance (percentage)	Investment income (dividends & interest) plus capital gains used for operations plus gifts and contributions plus net assets released from restrictions, divided by total expenses	Measures the amount of expenses funded by gifts and investment income
Return on net assets (percentage)	Net income divided by total assets	Traditional measure of "productivity" of an entity's asset base

Continued

Ratio Name	Calculation Method	Meaning and Use
II. Operating Results (continued)		
Investment income as percentage of operating income	Investment income (including unrealized gains), divided by total operating revenue	Demonstrates scale of annual endowment returns as percentage of the operating budget
III. Balance Sheet Strength		
Unrestricted resources-to-operations (percentage)	Total unrestricted net assets less net investment in plant, divided by total expenses	Measures the buffer provided to the annual operating budget by unrestricted expendable reserves
Expendable resources-to-operations (percentage)	Total unrestricted net assets plus total temporarily restricted net assets less net investment in plant, divided by total expenses	Measures the buffer provided to the annual operating budget by total expendable reserves
Average age of plant (years)	Accumulated depreciation divided by annual depreciation expense	Provides a crude indicator of institutional deferred maintenance and operating efficiency of existing plant facilities
IV. Leverage		
Debt service coverage	Net income plus depreciation and amortization plus interest expense, divided by annual debt service	Measures ability to pay debt service from operations
Unrestricted resources-to-debt (percentage)	Total unrestricted net assets less net investment in plant, divided by total outstanding debt	Measures the resources available to investors from unrestricted expendable reserves
Total resources-to-debt (percentage)	Total net assets less net investment in plant, divided by total outstanding debt	A broad measure of resources-to-debt that includes the corpus of endowed contributions

the state of scientific equipment to ensure laboratories are not outdated.

Funding Capital Projects Through Debt Financing. Trustees often are uncomfortable using debt financing to pay for capital projects because they fear saddling the institution and future boards with burdensome debt payments. Yet in their own businesses, they understand the importance of using debt strategically, and they know how to leverage their company's balance sheet. Part of this fear is a misunderstanding of stewardship and fiduciary responsibility. Many trustees believe that being a steward of the institution's assets prohibits borrowing to maintain those assets. This concern is understandable

Many trustees regard the institution's bond rating as a proxy for its financial condition.

and admirable, but not practical or appropriate. Colleges and universities need to use all their assets to the fullest extent. If one asset is a strong balance sheet that permits the issuance of tax-exempt bonds, then a bond issue should be weighed against other financing alternatives.

Obviously, no responsible board would issue long-term debt for short-term projects (such as balancing a current operating budget) even if it were possible to do so. Nor would it issue

debt for capital projects that could be funded through gifts. But it is prudent to issue debt for essential capital projects that are not likely candidates for capital gifts, such as upgrading the institution's infrastructure.

The simple math is compelling. Say $20 million is needed for infrastructure improvements. The board has two options: either to use $20 million from the institution's endowment with a total return of 15 percent or to issue 30-year, tax-exempt bonds with an interest rate of 7.5 percent. Responsible fiduciaries would choose the latter.

All the same, the decision to issue tax-exempt bonds should not be taken lightly. It is not free money. Boards must make certain the capital projects being funded through debt financing are essential to the institution's present and future. They also should understand the impact of servicing the debt on the operating budget.

• Which capital projects will be financed through debt?

• What is the institution's debt capacity?

• What rating is the institution likely to receive from rating agencies?

• Should the debt be fixed or variable?

• Will debt service be paid from the operating budget or from the endowment?

• Will the bond have "puts and call" provisions? (A "put" is an option to sell, and a "call" is an option to demand repayment of a loan on a bond issue.)

• Who will be the underwriter? (This should be a staff decision, not a board decision.)

Issuing debt requires a great deal of work, especially by the staff. Tax-exempt bonds usually are issued through a state agency that serves as the state's bond authority. In Massachusetts, for example, two state agencies are authorized to rate and issue bonds for colleges and universities. Although many public colleges and universities can issue debt directly, others (like their counterparts in the private sector) cannot.

Typically, institutional leaders engage a team of advisers to work on the bond issuance. The team includes the college's external counsel, auditors, bond counsel, investment advisers, underwriters, and a bank to serve as trustee. The issuance of a bond is similar to having a major medical checkup, where every part of your body is poked, prodded, and scrutinized by outside experts. If you get a clean bill of health, you feel great, but the checkup itself can be stressful.

Sometimes the board chair or vice chair will participate in the "bond issuance due-diligence meeting," at which every statement of fact contained in the offering statement, the loan and trust agreement, and the continuing disclosure is reviewed. It is good practice for at least the chair of the finance or budget committee to be present. All external advisers should attend this meeting to ensure that their representations to the potential bond buyers are accurate.

Next come Standards and Poor's and Moody's Investment Service, the external rating agencies that rate the bonds for investment quality. Officials of these agencies will review all of the documentation, including past financial reports, admissions statistics, student retention, fund-raising achievements, and outside accreditation reports. They also may visit the campus to interview management in order to make an independent assessment of the management team. They often want to speak directly with the board chair and the chair of the finance committee. Many trustees regard the institution's bond rating as a proxy for its financial condition.

Rating agencies consider several factors in determining a bond rating— usually the same factors boards track as strategic indicators of the institution's financial health. The factors include market demand, operating results, strength of the balance sheet, and leverage. Specifically, rating agencies seek ratio analysis in each of several key areas. The chart on pages 78 and 79 shows several bond-rating considerations.

Recommended Readings

Capital Formation Alternatives in Higher Education, National Association of College and University Business Officers. NACUBO Capital Management Series, 1988.

"College and University Financial Statements Under SFAS Nos. 116 and 117," by John Augustine. In the *Journal of Financial Statement Analysis*, Summer 1996.

"Debt Financing and Management," by Eva Klein and John H. Augustine. In *College and University Business Administration*, 6th ed. NACUBO, 2000.

"Managing the Facilities Portfolio: A Practical Approach to Institutional Facility Renewal and Deferred Maintenance," by Sean Rush and Applied Management Engineering. NACUBO, 1991.

NACUBO Guide to Issuing and Managing Debt, by George A. King, Richard E. Anderson, David M. Cygnowski, and Patrick J. Hennigan. NACUBO, 1994.

Planning and Managing Higher Education Facilities, by Harvey Kaiser. New Directions for Institutional Research, No 61. Jossey-Bass Publishers, 1989.

Ratio Analysis In Higher Education, 2nd ed. KPMG Peat Marwick, 1987.

C H A P T E R   7

CONTAINING COSTS

Regardless of the size, type, mission, or wealth of a college or university, the governing board should work hard to contain costs. Several factors help explain why. Students, families, taxpayers, and elected officials are demanding restraint on tuition increases. At the same time, institutions are being called on to provide greater financial aid, which reduces the institution's net tuition and, hence, its bottom line. And the ever-rising demands of students and faculty for more and better information technology, campus services, and laboratory equipment continue to compete for funding.

The responsibility for addressing cost issues falls squarely on the shoulders of the administration, with support from the board. Less clear is who within the administration has primary responsibility to deal with these difficult issues. If decision making is centralized, then strategies for reducing costs can be worked out by the senior staff. In a decentralized organization, however, the tough decisions that accompany cost reductions are largely in the hands of the schools or departments.

The desire for efficiency almost always collides with organizational structures designed to preserve the status quo. Most colleges and universities simply are not financially efficient organizations.

Ironically, when a faculty's reputation and stature nationally and regionally is strong, an institution's costs generally are higher. Bright, dedicated faculty generate creative ideas—new ways to teach, new avenues of research, new courses to add, and new fields and ideas to explore. They create a constant drumbeat of improvement that resonates across every aspect of a campus—classrooms, laboratories, residence halls, athletics facilities, and student-life halls. Creative faculty members and others in the academy seem to put forth an infinite number of ideas on how to improve their institutions. But institutions have a finite amount of money, and presidents and chief financial officers must produce balanced budgets, worry about long-term trends, communicate realistic financial messages to the campus, arbitrate among competing demands, stretch every dollar, and strive to maintain morale—all while being able to say No. These are challenging and thankless tasks.

How can the board help? One of the most important responsibilities of the board is to help frame the issue of cost containment by adopting financial policies that support long-range decision making and by persuading the campus community to view costs and the importance of cost containment in the same ways.

Absent a fiscal crisis, the campus community will not respond to prolonged discussions about containing costs. When things are going well, everyone assumes that if the status quo is maintained, things will continue to go well. When long-range projections predict deficits, the first response is to challenge the assumptions on which the projections were built. The second response is to argue that the problem is not one of expenditures, but rather a lack of revenue growth. Simply put, the issue is redefined as a revenue problem, not an expense problem.

Through well-researched data (including appropriate benchmarks with peer institutions) and good, old-fashioned jawboning, the board can help define cost issues and help administrators convince the campus that certain institutional conditions must change to avoid deficits. The hard work begins

when a president or chief financial officer, working with the president's cabinet or a budget advisory group, designs a process for making decisions about where to make cuts. In the ideal world, such decisions would be made rationally, using a process that involves all elements of the community. In the world of higher education, however, the most difficult decisions are made by a handful of senior administrators.

Depending on the severity of cost pressures, institutional leaders may use three approaches to reduce costs. Administrators often will employ one or more of these approaches simultaneously.

1. Temporary Solutions. The first budget administrators face usually has a deficit. Departmental requests are certain to exceed budget guidelines for various reasons: One department wants to launch a new initiative; another wants additional staff; utility expenses unexpectedly may rise; and everyone wants more computers. During the budget-making process, administrators can address most of these issues, yet still face a deficit.

An institution's fixed costs usually consume all the incremental revenue generated through tuition increases, new gifts, and increased support from the endowment. Growth in salaries and fringe benefits, financial aid, and inflationary adjustments to nonpersonnel budgets leave little revenue, if any, for innovation or new programs. The typical college budget has no flexibility. This is a simple economic fact of life in

Absent a fiscal crisis, the campus community will not respond to prolonged discussions about containing costs.

higher education: High fixed costs devour institutions' incremental or discretionary revenue. If the institution still runs a deficit after all the "arm wrestling" is complete, administrators may apply various temporary solutions.

• *Making across-the-board cuts.* This approach is mindless, but it works in the short term. Someone with authority—usually the president, chief financial officer, or a senior person on a budget advisory committee—mandates that all departments reduce their budgets by a specific amount. Every department then determines how to achieve the reduction. This approach generates a fair amount of grumbling, and some departments raise legitimate issues, which often are ignored, lest one department be favored over another.

• *Freezing salaries.* Because salaries account for a high proportion of expenditures, they are logical places to start cutting costs. Although this strategy is logical and obvious, it is extremely difficult and cannot be used very often. Freezing salaries can bring a budget into balance, but it does not address underlying long-term, systemic issues. No administrator takes pleasure in freezing salaries.

• *Freezing positions.* Other ways to save salaries include not filling open positions or capping the total number of positions available. These two solutions require existing staff members to take on additional work. Without restructuring work loads, a hiring freeze is a temporary measure, at best.

• *Reducing capital expenditures.* Institutional leaders also can decide to stop spending money on capital purchases or to delay purchases longer than they would under optimum conditions. If the normal replacement cycle for desktop computers is every three years, for example, college officials may extended the cycle to four or five years. They may delay purchasing scientific equipment or updating laboratories a year or two. This solution creates a backlog that eventually must be addressed. Further, the amount of actual savings can be deceptive. Older computers and equipment often require more maintenance, for example.

• *Reducing major maintenance.* This approach, unfortunately, is common. Delaying the replacement of equipment or postponing maintenance of buildings and campus infrastructure simply transfers the expense from one year to the next. The board can "buy" an additional year or two by extending the replacement cycle on equipment or by letting the campus deteriorate a little, but it should be wary about a cost-containment policy that relies too readily on this approach.

2. Mid-Term Solutions. If budget pressures persist beyond temporary solutions, officials must introduce a second level of remedies. These solutions begin to address structural deficits, at least marginally. While such measures are not radical, they can have lasting, albeit modest, results.

• *Redesigning administrative processes.* When a budget requires deep or permanent reductions, administrative areas become likely candidates. The desire to find savings in administration is natural and logical—administrative departments are not the core units of the enterprise. After all, students do not enroll in a college or university because it has a terrific finance office.

Finding savings in administration usually begins by examining existing processes. Which processes can be streamlined? How will the work be redistributed? How many staff positions can be eliminated, if any?

These studies ultimately reveal steps, procedures, or processes that are unnecessary and can be eliminated with little or no reduction in quality or service. They create streamlined processes that serve students and others better, reduce bureaucracy, and make better use of technology.

• *Reengineering.* Reengineering is the fundamental rethinking and radical redesign of business processes to bring about dramatic improvement in performance, according to management consultant Michael Hammer, credited as the father of the reengineering movement. Many trustees are familiar with reengineering as a cost-cutting measure because it is commonly practiced with

success in the private sector. In higher education, many major research universities have gone through significant reengineering efforts, but the jury is still out on whether the results justify the time and cost expended. Universities have reported major improvements in some business practices, but few have reported radical redesign or significant savings. Consequently, trustees who have witnessed reengineering success in the private sector but who see an inconsistent track record in the academy often become frustrated.

Why does reengineering work well in corporations and not so well in higher education? First, there simply is too much resistance to change in colleges and universities. And second, power and loyalty in academe are dispersed in departments and subunits. For reengineering to be successful, it must be driven from the topmost levels of an organization. That's the rub. In higher education, institutional leaders can find it hard going to achieve systemwide acceptance of anything, let alone a reengineering effort in the loosely coupled structure of the academy.

• *Outsourcing.* Outsourcing, an important element in redesigning processes, has the dual goal of increasing efficiency while reducing costs. With the growth of service providers that serve higher education, many administrative functions can be outsourced, from food service to groundskeeping to residence-hall management. Determining true savings, however, is not an easy calculation. Financial officers must consider several variables, not the least of which are the effect on staff morale and the resulting political fallout. Some institutions have created successful partnerships with nearby institutions on certain business functions.

• *Growing through substitution.* Because most colleges have a limit on the number of students they can accommodate, they cannot pay for rising expenses or add programs by increasing student enrollment. Theoretically, to add a new program, institutional leaders should eliminate an existing program. In other words, institutions should grow by substitution.

Many institutional leaders claim to practice growth through substitution. In reality, however, most have perfected the growth side of this equation, but few have figured out how to terminate academic programs. The fact is, institutional leaders should devote as much time and energy to deciding which programs to drop as they do to which to add. Certainly, low-enrollment programs or majors should be candidates, but there may be good reasons to use other criteria. Institutional missions are important frames of reference in these matters. The budgeting process must examine both sides of the drop-add equation if an institution is to check the growth of embedded costs.

3. Permanent Changes. Serious planning begins when the pressure to control costs reaches a critical point—the point where fundamental, structural change is essential. The board is responsible for ensuring such planning takes place. Wise presidents and boards will not do this planning in isolation. A budget advisory committee or a committee that includes representatives from several groups should be part of the process.

How to begin? The board can help determine what information is needed to make informed decisions. Benchmark studies of peer institutions can help answer two initial questions: (1) Where are we out of sync financially with our peers, and (2) what areas have recently grown the most?

Some institutions gather data by conducting activity-based cost studies, which provide detailed information on the cost of all major activities. Be forewarned, however: An activity-based accounting study is an enormous undertaking and should not be entered into lightly. It may be worth the effort, however. One important benefit is that it can awaken the campus community to the cost of doing business. Armed with data about the cost of various activities, an advisory committee can begin to form an approach for structural changes to contain costs.

Regardless of the specific recommendations from an advisory committee, the board should expect them to be controversial. Change does not come peacefully or without opposition in academic institutions, especially permanent change. Some examples of permanent change follow:

• *Identifying expensive policies.* A review of expensive policies is worthy of consideration because it focuses the discussion on policies, rather than on departments or individuals. (Wise financial officers advise trustees to understand their institution's most expensive policies thoroughly even if the institution is not in financial crisis.) Although the phrase "expensive policies" can raise hackles among some individuals, discovering these policies has strategic value. Trustees and others should first identify the institution's expensive policies and then ask these questions: (1) Is this policy central to our mission? (2) Is it an important institutional priority? (3) Can it be changed?

At one private college, the budget advisory committee, working with the budget office, developed a comprehensive list of expensive policies. (Some committee members found the term so offensive they changed it to "valued policies.") As the list was shared with the wider community, policies were added. Students were particularly helpful in identifying policies and practices they considered expensive. A partial list follows:

• Need-blind admissions and a commitment to meeting the full needs of admitted students.

• A student-to-faculty ratio of 10 to 1.

• Budgeted enrollments of 2,180 students, which limited the number of first-year students and transfer students the college could admit, even though the campus could accommodate more.

• Dining halls in individual dorms.

• An on-campus post office and printing service.

• No limit to the number of students participating in foreign study and exchange programs.

• Overly generous student-support services, including an on-campus health-service facility.

• Aggressive compensation objectives.

• Annual salary increases for faculty and staff.

• Inefficient class scheduling (too few students scheduled during winter session, few evening classes, and underutilized classrooms during off-peak hours).

• A very high standard of building maintenance.

• A commitment to providing juniors and seniors with single rooms.

• A commitment to a multicultural campus, which determines many policies and practices in student recruitment, faculty and staff hiring, and programming.

• A commitment to maintain certain academic departments that have low enrollments.

• Generous employee benefit plans, such as pension plans, college contributions to employee health insurance, and benefits for part-time employees.

• A strong commitment to technology in administration, classrooms, research laboratories, the library, and the campus network, with associated training and programming.

• Expansion of global outreach and programming.

Such lists touch every aspect of an institution.

Trustees often ask what makes policies expensive. Should a policy that is efficient and costs less than at a peer institution be considered expensive? The answer is Yes. The point of such studies is to explore "effectiveness," not "efficiency."

How important is a certain policy to the core mission of the institution? Not everyone agrees, of course, but this question helps inform discussion and keeps it focused on fundamental values and effectiveness. Changes in any expensive policy can be profound and are likely to result in substantial cost savings.

The process of conducting such a study is time consuming but enlightening and useful. It takes hard work to calculate the actual cost of the policy and weigh its value against that cost. Some policies do not need much discussion because they are so fundamental to the mission and culture of the college; others require a great deal of study and thought. Judging the effect of a policy change is difficult. In the end, a few expensive policies may actually be changed, and others will become candidates for a second review, depending on the urgency of the institution's financial circumstances.

• *Making draconian cuts.* If a college faces financial issues so severe that its very existence is threatened, it must take radical, permanent, and often-draconian measures. There simply is no other choice.

How decisions are made under these perilous conditions depends on the culture of the institution, the personal style and professional strength of the president, the degree of ownership by and direction from the board, and the severity of the crisis. Such decisions often involve reducing the payroll by

Everyone should understand the current reality, and hard data must back up the financial projections.

eliminating functions as well as positions, a move often referred to as "rightsizing."

Trustees really earn their stripes when they serve on a board of an institution that faces financial exigency. How a board responds to the crisis is critical and goes right to the heart of what being a fiduciary is all about. Presidential and board leadership will be tested, and the board and the president must stand shoulder to shoulder before the college community.

What does a board have to do? First, the board leadership and the president have to be in agreement on the severity of the problem. There can be no wishful thinking. Everyone should understand the current reality, and hard data must back up the financial projections. A plan must be developed that addresses the systemic issues as well as the process the institution is contemplating to correct course. The board and senior staff should discuss these plans diligently and deliberately before publicizing them.

A special committee of the board should be formed to monitor progress and to provide advice and counsel to the president. The college community should be fully aware of the situation and have confidence that the plan is realistic and will work. In the final analysis, the college community will have to implement the plan and live with the consequences. The chances of success are greatly improved if all constituents unite behind the plan and can work together in a positive, determined manner. Maintaining morale during these times is not easy, and the board can help by providing the community with calm, reasoned, and strong guidance.

To make staff reductions permanent, institutional leaders must identify the functions the institution no longer can perform or provide. Staff-reduction programs must be accompanied by altering expectations of the degree and level of service formerly provided. Careful planning is essential. The positions cannot be eliminated on a voluntarily basis. Early retirement programs do not work because the "wrong" people may leave. If the campus community continues to expect the same level and quality of services, it also will expect the positions to be restored over time. The institution will have gone through a very painful exercise without gaining any lasting benefit.

Another draconian cut is to eliminate programs or whole departments. This decision is the most difficult, although it is the most permanent and effective. Obviously, it requires strong and courageous leadership.

Sometimes, this approach is the only alternative. Such bold action can lead to a turnaround in the financial health of the institution. There are several

examples of where effective leadership, coupled with a willingness to drop programs, reduce staff, and shrink the institution's size, has led to remarkable recoveries in financial health. Institutional chief executives are likely to know the names of colleges that recently have achieved such turnarounds.

Elements of Cost Containment. The most important question governing boards must address is what cost-containment approaches are most effective in reducing costs and least damaging to educational quality. It makes sense to improve efficiency and eliminate redundancies. It also makes sense to develop good benchmarks for comparison and to gather data on areas or functions that seem inefficient. And it is important to examine an institution's expensive policies so everyone understands the costs and benefits of the policies.

Institutional leaders should make a commitment to work on several fronts at once, and the board must be clear in its intent to do everything possible to make the cost of education affordable.

The following vignette may be instructive: A small private college preparing for a reaccreditation process conducted a careful analysis of its efforts to constrain the growth rate of expenses. The chief financial officer lamented to the visiting committee that he was being criticized for emphasizing the importance of cost containment too much. The campus community no longer was paying attention. One of the visiting team members offered this helpful—and obvious—insight. People were tired of hearing about "cost containment," especially when everything was going so well. She suggested the term "funding priorities" be used instead.

People can get excited about discussing funding priorities, even if they disagree about what they are. It is a much more effective way to engage the community thoughtfully about where the institution should invest and where it should cut back. This change of vocabulary can make a difficult and contentious conversation positive and engaging.

(*Note: This chapter is adapted from the author's discussion in* Roles and Responsibilities of the Chief Financial Officer, *edited by Lucie Lapovsky and Mary P. McKeown-Moak. Jossey-Bass Publishers, 1999.*)

Recommended Readings

"The Constraints on Campus Productivity," by Robert Birnbaum. Chapter 2 in *Productivity and Higher Education*, edited by Richard Anderson and Joel W. Meyerson. The Forum for College Financing, Peterson's Guides, 1992.

"Improvement Strategies for Administrative and Support Services," by William F. Massy. Chapter 3 in *Productivity and Higher Education*, edited by Richard Anderson and Joel W. Meyerson. The Forum for College Financing, Peterson's Guides, 1992.

Managing Change in Higher Education, by Douglas Steeples. Jossey-Bass Publishers, 1990.

Managing a Comprehensive Change Effort, by L. Edwin Coate. NACUBO, 1995.

Practical Approaches to Rightsizing, NACUBO, 1992.

Wise Moves in Hard Times—Creating and Managing Resilient Colleges and Universities, by David W. Leslie and E.K. Fretwell, Jr. Jossey-Bass Publishers, 1996.

CHAPTER 8

Building Trust and Transparency Through the Audit Process

The board of trustees is held to a high standard of full financial disclosure, transparency, and accountability. These standards are the bedrock of fiduciary responsibility.

"Transparency" may seem like an odd term to describe a board responsibility. In this context, it refers to (1) the clarity of an institution's financial condition and the subsequent ability of the general public and students and their parents to "see" and understand it and (2) the ability of the faculty, alumni, benefactors, and other friends of the institution to assess its relative health. If an institution's financial condition is transparent, individuals are able to make informed investment decisions.

Transparency also means the institution's stakeholders will appreciate the leadership's openness to engender trust. Given the complexity of higher education accounting conventions,

creating financial reports that are transparent and understandable to lay individuals is a major challenge.

The Work of the Audit Committee. The audit committee's work centers on ensuring the institution is an effective steward of resources, honors donors' restrictions, follows contract provisions, and publishes accurate, reliable financial information. The committee does not set policy, but it helps ensure that policies are carried out.

An audit committee should have a small number of members, generally not more than four or five trustees. If the committee is too large, it becomes difficult to have the detailed, intense discussions that often are necessary. If the committee is too small, individual members can become overwhelmed. Committee members must be financially literate, experienced, and comfortable in discussing accounting issues. Most important is their ability to ask probing questions and recognize the significance of issues independent auditors may raise.

The more experienced an audit committee chair, the more effective the committee. Chairs should have broad experience with complex organizations with large budgets. Their personal style should engender respect and confidence. They should shun dysfunctional politeness in the presence of staff and auditors. The most effective chairs encourage committee members to ask good questions and respect staff without shirking their duties and responsibilities on behalf of the governing boards they serve.

The Audit Calendar. Most audit committees operate within similar cycles. In March or April, the audit firm will send the committee a proposed "scope of work" that outlines the areas the audit will cover and the timetable in which the audit will occur. The scope of work will propose special areas to be audited on a rotating basis. The audit may take a special look, for example, at travel reimbursements, the handling of petty cash, the reconciliation of bank statements, or the installation of a new financial software package. It is common for the committee each year to suggest a special focus on a different area that is not routinely audited. (See table on page 95.)

The scope of work often will contain a fee proposal, which can lead to interesting discussions on the number of hours required to perform various parts of the audit. Audit fees tend to increase at a rate much greater than the increase in the Consumer Price Index. Committees should pay attention to the fee proposal and, if necessary, take a firm position on the rate of increase. This matter often is decided within the larger context of how long a given auditor has served the institution.

There are no hard-and-fast rules, but a sound principle is for auditors to be changed at some appropriate interval. The committee should decide and recommend this interval to the board. Using the same audit team for more than five years probably is not advisable; a different team every two years also may be unwise. However, frequent turnover in the team of auditors can bring heavy costs to the institution because of the steep learning curve in understanding an institution's financial operations. Different auditors bring different styles and operating insights— and this is a good thing.

The scope of work also lists the team members who will perform the audit. This is especially important because most financial officers want some continuity in the audit team. It takes a great deal of staff time to instruct the auditors on the financial software the college uses and on where to find information. Nevertheless, audit teams tend to change from year to year. Consequently, changing audit firms periodically may not be as disruptive as one might think. The change of personnel on the audit team also ensures that the team members themselves will not become too closely aligned with management.

The basic objective of the audit is to express an opinion on the institution's financial statements. The audit will be done in accordance with generally accepted auditing standards to ensure the financial statements are presented

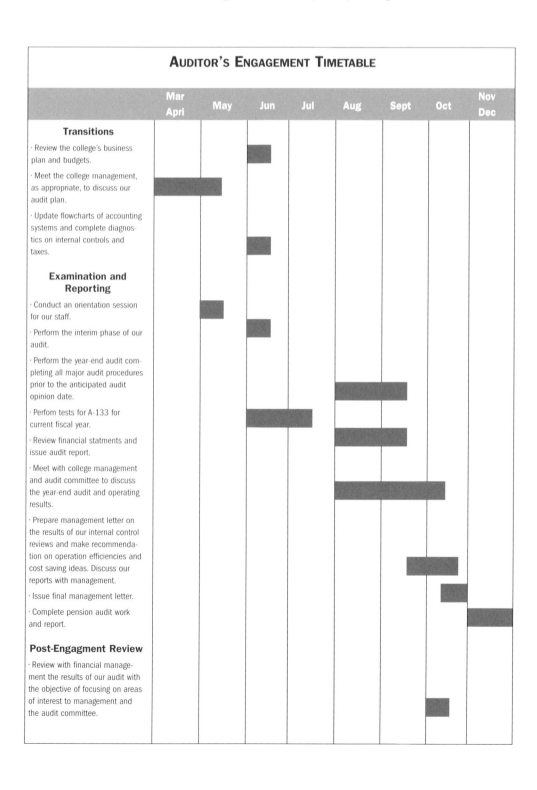

AUDITOR'S ENGAGEMENT TIMETABLE								
	Mar Apri	May	Jun	Jul	Aug	Sept	Oct	Nov Dec
Transitions								
· Review the college's business plan and budgets.			▮					
· Meet the college management, as appropriate, to discuss our audit plan.	▮▮							
· Update flowcharts of accounting systems and complete diagnostics on internal controls and taxes.			▮					
Examination and Reporting								
· Conduct an orientation session for our staff.		▮						
· Perform the interim phase of our audit.			▮					
· Perform the year-end audit completing all major audit procedures prior to the anticipated audit opinion date.					▮▮			
· Perfom tests for A-133 for current fiscal year.			▮▮					
· Review financial statments and issue audit report.					▮▮			
· Meet with college management and audit committee to discuss the year-end audit and operating results.					▮▮▮			
· Prepare management letter on the results of our internal control reviews and make recommendation on operation efficiencies and cost saving ideas. Discuss our reports with management.							▮	
· Issue final management letter.							▮	
· Complete pension audit work and report.								▮
Post-Engagment Review								
· Review with financial management the results of our audit with the objective of focusing on areas of interest to management and the audit committee.							▮	

in accordance with generally accepted accounting principles. The auditors will try to determine whether the financial statements are free of material misstatements and whether the financial statements present fairly the institution's financial position, results of operations, and changes in net assets and cash flows. To do so, auditors examine, on a test basis, evidence supporting the amounts and disclosures in the financial statements, assess the accounting principles used and the estimates made by management, and evaluate the effectiveness of the overall financial presentation.

Audits are based on the concept of selective testing of the data underlying financial statements, which involves judgments regarding the areas to be tested. When the scope of work is presented to the audit committee, committee members often discuss what areas will be tested and the extent of the testing. The committee must be comfortable with the judgments and understand the depth of testing required to render an opinion. The auditors will monitor financial-control issues and report serious matters to the committee.

Executive Sessions. As a routine matter, the outside auditors should meet with the audit committee privately, without institutional management. This enables trustees and the auditors to talk candidly about the effectiveness of the institution's financial management. *The Report and Recommendations of the Blue Ribbon Committee on Improving the Effectiveness of Corporate Audit Committees*, published

by the New York Stock Exchange and the National Association of Securities Dealers, describes the importance of routine private sessions:

> The audit committee should develop regularly scheduled meetings with the outside auditors independent of management. Only through open, regular, frank, and confidential dialogue will the audit committee be in a position to utilize the knowledge of the outside auditors in assessing internal controls, management, the internal auditor, and the impact of each on the quality and reliability of financial statements.

If an internal auditor is chosen to conduct the institution's audit, he or she should meet with the audit committee chair routinely and with the entire committee periodically. To discharge its responsibilities effectively, the audit committee must be satisfied that it has access to all information it needs, unfettered by management's desire to put the best face on issues. The Blue Ribbon Committee also addressed the difficult role of an internal auditor. Although its comments are directed toward profit-making enterprises, they apply equally well to nonprofit organizations:

> The internal auditor occupies a unique position—he or she is "employed" by management, but is also expected to review the conduct of management. This can create significant tension since the internal

auditor's "independence" from management is necessary for the auditor to objectively assess management's actions, but the auditor's "dependence" on management for employment is clear. Recognizing this tension, the committee believes that it is essential to have formal mechanisms in place to facilitate confidential exchanges between the internal auditor and the audit committee.

The Concept of Materiality. "Materiality" is an important concept in auditing. Determining what is material—and therefore worth reporting—is a judgment call. The standard auditors apply is that accounting information is material if "the judgment of a reasonable person relying on the information would have been changed or influenced by the omission or misstatement." Management and the auditors can disagree about whether an issue is material. An item that may be material for one institution may not be material for another. If an institution has a very large endowment, it is hard to reach the materiality threshold. A poorly endowed school may have a more difficult time arguing that an audit finding is not material.

Public Responsibilities of Private Auditors. One of the ironies for an independent college is that its independent auditors are required to perform audits for the federal government. They must follow strict guidelines in auditing pension plans, federal financial-aid programs, and government research

grants. The Office of Management and Budget (OMB) Circular A-133 requires auditors of independent institutions to obtain an understanding of internal controls over major federal programs and to report any shortcomings.

Government auditing standards require auditors to prepare a written report on the tests they conduct to determine compliance with applicable laws and regulations. This report will contain "all instances of noncompliance that are material to the financial statements." From management's perspective, this part of the audit can produce headaches. It is almost impossible not to have some item reported (such as an incomplete file), even though the item may not be "material" to management. When a "noncompliance" is identified and reported, a long and tedious process sometimes ensues.

Major research universities often have federal auditors resident on their campus because they receive such large sums for federally sponsored research projects. And state universities and colleges have to answer to state auditors as well. Most colleges and universities that have significant outside funding or complex organizational structures have an internal audit function. The internal auditor is used both as an internal check that procedures are followed (the watchdog function) and as a source for benchmarking good management practices. The internal auditor frequently has a direct reporting line to the chair of the audit committee.

STATEMENT OF FINANCIAL POSITION
FOR THE YEARS ENDED JUNE 30, 2000 AND 1999 (IN THOUSANDS)

	2000	1999
Assets		
Cash and cash equivalents	$14,866	$15,650
Accounts receivable, net	1,010	851
Short-term investments	11,933	11,327
Inventories	1,109	1,062
Prepaid expenses and other assets	2,130	2,148
Pledges receivables, net	15,333	15,285
Student loans receivable, net	2,716	2,764
Long-term investments, at market	249,152	240,211
Land, buildings, and equipment, net	109,626	96,211
Total assets	$407,935	$386,041
Liabilities		
Accounts payable and accrued expenses	5,903	7,188
Deposits and deferred revenue	2,897	2,759
Postretirement benefits	6,312	6,029
Federal student loan funds	2,831	2,782
Long-term debt	48,579	49,720
Total liabilities	66,522	68,478
Net Assets		
Unrestricted	157,212	147,342
Temporarily restricted	103,537	93,522
Permanently restricted	80,664	76,699
Total net assets	341,413	317,563
Total liabilities and net assets	$407,935	$386,041

Telling Your Institution's Financial Story.
An educational institution is required to publish an annual financial statement. The minimum requirement includes the independent auditor's opinion letter, financial statement footnotes, and three schedules—the Statement of Activities, the Statement of Financial Position, and the Statement of Cash Flows. (A sample Statement of Activities appears on page 8; samples of the latter two statements appear on pages 98 and 100.)

Under recent guidelines of the Financial Accounting Standards Board, these reports are easier to understand because previous financial accounting statements and ensuing public reports were based on fund-accounting principles. For many, however, even these improved financial statements can be opaque. One has to be fairly adept at reading nonprofit financial statements to get a clear picture of an institution's financial health. Again, AGB's *Understanding Financial Statements* offers help for officials of private institutions. (For public institutions, the Governmental Accounting Standards Accounting Board established guidelines similar to those from FASB; new requirements take effect for fiscal years beginning June 15, 2001.)

Annual financial reports serve various functions and have various audiences, and the audit committee should be concerned with all of them— especially how information is presented to specific audiences. As internal documents, annual financial reports are designed to inform the campus community of the institution's financial condition. As external documents for various rating agencies, the holders of the institution's bonds, and accrediting agencies, these reports usually are required to be filed with states' attorneys general offices. In addition, annual reports often are used as fund-raising documents for major donors who want to know how their contributions are being managed.

Implementation of the new FASB accounting rules caused some institutions to show operating deficits in their first year or so of use. This kind of adverse impact on the balance sheet and audit report can be addressed in the chief financial officer's letter in the insti-

tution's annual report accompanying the financial statement. This letter also can temper exceptionally good news, such as unusually high endowment returns.

Many colleges and universities put great effort into telling their financial stories. To publish only the statements of Financial Position, Activities, and Cash Flows and Footnotes is to fall short of producing clear and transparent reports. Annual reports commonly publish supplemental financial charts, graphs, and tables to help readers understand financial statements. Pie charts show the sources of revenue and expenses; other graphs show the rate of tuition growth; bar charts might display endowment performance over time; and still other charts illustrate the difference between tuition and the true cost to educate a student.

One liberal arts college consistently publishes a list of key financial indicators for ten-year periods to help readers see long-term trends. The college's annual report includes such indicators as the number of students, revenues versus expenses, total giving to the college, the number of alumni who contribute to the institution, the number of employees, the student-to-faculty ratio, the amount of deferred maintenance, and so on.

These data put the current year in a historical context and help readers see the basic financial condition of the institution. As audit committee members review the institution's annual financial report, they should pay close attention to two nonfinancial factors: First, can

STATEMENT OF CASH FLOWS
FOR THE YEARS ENDED JUNE 30, 2000 AND 1999 (IN THOUSANDS)

	2000	1999
Cash Flows From Operating Activities		
Change in net assets	$23,850	$22,510
Adjustments to reconcile change in net assets to net cash provided by operating activities:		
Depreciation and amortization	4,684	3,866
Gains and investments	(15,585)	(2,756)
Gain on equipment disposals	(99)	(63)
Capital Gifts	(5,886)	(7,151)
Other nonoperating activity	1,698	257
Changes in assets and liabilities that provide (use) cash:		
Accounts receivable	(159)	(71)
Pledges receivable	(48)	(15,285)
Student loans receivable	48	46
Short-term investments	(666)	(221)
Inventories	(47)	(56)
Prepaid expenses and other assets	65	(74)
Accounts payable and accrued expenses	(1,285)	1,594
Deposits and deferred revenues	138	165
Postretirement benefits	283	6,029
Other Changes	18	(1,478)
Net cash provided by operating activities	6,749	7,312
Cash Flows From Investing Activities		
Purchases of plant and equipment, net	(18,016)	(18,909)
Purchases of investments	(265,934)	(337,735)
Proceeds from sales and maturities of investments	273,370	336,969
Other nonoperating activity	(1,698)	(257)
Net cash used in investing activities	(12,278)	(19,932)
Cash Flows From Financing Activities		
Proceeds from contributions for:		
Investment in endowment	3,965	4,851
Investment in long-lived assets	1,921	2,300
Proceeds from issuance of long-term debt		
Payments on long-term debt	(1,141)	(1,068)
Net cash provided by financing activities	4,745	6,083
Net decrease in cash and cash equivalents	(784)	(6,537)
Cash and cash equivalents, beginning of year	15,650	22,187
Cash and cash equivalents, end of year	$14,886	$15,650
Supplemental Data		
Noncash investing and financing activities–gifts in kind	$412	$580
Interest paid	$2,952	$2,114

average readers understand it? Second, does it portray an accurate and complete story about how the college uses its resources and manages its finances?

Risk Management. Traditionally, the audit committee is responsible to the governing board for overseeing the institution's risk-management program. Risk management often is defined as making sure an institution carries adequate insurance to cover negligence suits and property losses. That's a good beginning. Unfortunately, in today's litigious world, an institution's exposure to risk must be seen in a broader context. Institutions are exposed to the following four basic types of risk:

1. *Operating risk.* This includes a weather catastrophe or a fire that disrupts teaching or research for an extended period or makes significant facilities unusable.

2. *Legal and regulatory risk.* This includes litigation by employees or students claiming discrimination or failure to comply with environmental or Occupational Safety and Health Administration (OSHA) requirements.

3. *Financial risk.* This can include such things as a sudden drop in tuition revenue, an investment loss caused by imprudent trading, or loss of significant support from donors, government agencies, or corporate sponsors.

4. *Political or reputational risk.* This type of risk, although less common, can take the form of a loss of accreditation or favorable bond rating, sanctions from the National Collegiate Athletic

Association (NCAA), or negative publicity caused by a crime on campus.

The increase in litigation involving higher education is staggering. A 1998 survey by Tillinghast Towers Perrin on educators' legal liability found a continuing escalation in the frequency, spread, and total cost of claims. Annual claim frequency at public institutions rose from 1.1 claims to 5 claims in a five-year period. Claim frequency at private institutions rose from .84 claims to 1.80 claims in the same period. Average total costs nearly doubled, largely because of legal costs to defend institutions.

The increase in lawsuits is a direct result of changes in legislation that have stimulated more employment-related claims. The laws that have had the greatest influence on the increase in claims involving higher education are: the Older Workers Benefit Protection Act (1990), the Americans With Disabilities Act (1990), the Civil Rights Act of 1991, the Family and Medical Leave Act (1993), and an increased focus on Title IX of the 1972 Education Amendments.

Employment-related litigation takes a heavy toll—financially and in reputation—on academic institutions. It diverts valuable time and human resources from the institution's primary mission. Gerhard Casper, former president of Stanford University, spoke of the strain litigation places on individuals in an address to his university in 1998:

Beyond the diversion of a significant amount of money from core academic purposes, excessive legalism depletes valuable time. If depositions in a single case can consume 10 percent of a university president's official working hours during an entire quarter, and if dedicated university deans, faculty, and staff must accept being personally attacked by a plaintiff's lawyer for days on end, the effect on the individuals and the institution is debilitating indeed.

These days, and for the first time in my life, I myself am mostly a client (and a victim) of lawyers. A sobering experience! My daughter, who is a lawyer, when asked what her father does, answers: "My father? Oh, he is a defendant."

Confronted with the increase in risk exposure, audit committees should make sure management has developed and implemented a risk-management program. Institutional managers cannot eliminate risk, but they can identify its causes, types, and potential severity and then plan accordingly.

The audit committee needs to understand and approve the level of insurance coverage the institution carries. Its members should know which risks are covered and which are not. Further, the committee should ensure that risk-management program responsibility falls to a senior institutional administrator. Few academic institutions, with the exception of large universities, have full-time risk managers. The responsibility for risk management typically falls to an administrator who reports to the chief

financial officer. In some institutions, a combination of in-house administrators and risk-management consultants are accountable for an institution's program. In reality, no single person can manage the variety of risk an education institution faces. All managers, from supervisors in administrative departments to deans of the faculty, should be responsible for managing risks within their area.

Risk management is such a broad, diffuse, and potentially explosive area that the most effective oversight an audit committee can offer is to ask tough questions of management and to ensure it does not neglect risk management. By doing so, committee members can keep managers focused, encourage attention to risk-management processes, and provide objective governance input that may alert administrators to risks or issues in which individual trustees have professional or special expertise.

Other board committees may share oversight responsibility for risk management. The investment committee may develop policies on investment risk and the amount of the endowment that can be invested in derivatives or other "risky" investments. The long-range planning committee might evaluate an institution's strategic risks. But the audit committee has the primary responsibility for overseeing risk management for employment practices, operational and catastrophic exposures, campuswide litigation, and compliance with laws and regulations.

Audit committee members should receive a risk-management report from management that identifies the level and types of insurance coverage, self-insured or uninsured exposures, significant claims and losses, risk-management and loss-control initiatives, and other special issues. The format, content, and frequency of risk-management reports will vary according to the size and complexity of the institution. Regardless of the size of the enterprise, all colleges and universities should focus on their vulnerabilities to litigation and reduce exposures to risk through proactive initiatives.

Conflict of Interest. Audit committees usually are responsible for developing, implementing, and administering a board's conflict-of-interest policy. Every governing board should have a written conflict-of-interest policy. Fundamental to a trustee's "duty of loyalty" is his or her pledge not to take advantage of his or her position on an academic governing board for personal gain.

Conflict-of-interest policies differ among institutions, of course, but one common element is the requirement that all trustees annually disclose any real or potential conflict of interest. The audit committee reviews disclosure statements and recommends appropriate action to the board. Board meeting minutes should show that all potential conflicts of interest were disclosed and discussed and appropriate decisions made. Concurrently with this oversight, the audit committee should review the institution's relationship with significant vendors or service providers to ensure such relationships are in the institution's best interests.

Recommended Readings

Board Basics: "The Audit Committee," by John S. Ostrom. AGB, 1996.

Board Basics: "Essentials of Risk Management," by Burton Sonenstein and Laura Kumin. AGB, 1998.

"The Audit Committee: A Key to Financial Accountability in Nonprofit Organizations," by Sandra L. Johnson. National Center for Nonprofit Boards, 1995.

"Audit Committees—A Pivotal Role," Deloitte & Touche, LLP.

Audits of College & Universities, Accounting Standards Division, American Institute of Certified Public Accountants, 1999.

"Global Best Practices for Audit Committees," Arthur Anderson LLP. The Conference Board, 1998.

"Identifying and Managing Risk," by Janice Abraham, in *Roles and Responsibilities of the Chief Financial Officer*, edited by Lucie Lapovsky and Mary P. McKeown-Moak. Jossey-Bass Publishers, 1999.

Selecting an Auditor, by John S. Ostrom. NACUBO, 1992.

CHAPTER 9

Pulling It All Together

Governing boards are responsible for overseeing and protecting the institution's assets. Although trustees at times may feel overwhelmed by the complexities of the academic institution, no single trustee is expected to know everything about its financial intricacies. These responsibilities are shared collectively, and the work is divided among the trustees and the board's various standing committees. Trustees can exercise their financial responsibilities thoughtfully and effectively by ensuring a judicious number of trustees have relevant experience and expertise. They also need a thought process that emphasizes focusing on the right fiduciary issues at the right time.

Several themes concerning what it means to be a fiduciary appear throughout this book:

Academic institutions, of course, have *stake*holders, not *share*holders. The governing board, except in some church-sponsored institutions, is legally, ethically, and morally the "owner" of the institution. With the assumption of this responsibility comes the requirement to be the steward of the institution's financial, physical, and human assets. These assets have to be nurtured, protected, and used in a manner that is consistent with the institution's mission and values. The perspective of the trustees must be intergenerational, with equal concern for today's and tomorrow's students. Accordingly, the board is responsible for ensuring appropriate *due diligence* before major financial decisions are made.

An understanding of the institution's current reality is paramount. To gain this understanding, board members need data and documents that illuminate the campus as it exists today. This assessment should include a close examination of the following conditions:

• How attractive is the campus to prospective students, how well does it retain current students, and how satisfied are its graduates?

• What is the institution's comprehensive financial condition, and what are its major fiscal vulnerabilities and opportunities?

• What are the institution's competitive and comparative advantages and its core competencies?

• What are the strengths and qualities of peer institutions as well as those in its "aspirant" category?

It is important for trustees to have a firm grasp of their institution's vulnerabilities. Knowing what events could significantly harm the long-term viability of their institution is essential. It is impossible to plan for all catastrophic events, but knowing the nature of possible scenarios that could be especially harmful reflects favorably on the boards and its management. It is important to conceptualize and discuss contingency plans periodically.

It also is important for trustees to appreciate the major sources of revenue and what it takes to sustain them. A key to understanding the sustainability of revenue sources is to examine their growth rate over recent years and to make assumptions about their future growth rate and the conditions under which they might increase or decrease.

Institutions that will thrive in the future are likely to be those with the greatest financial flexibility. Financial flexibility enables an institution to change with the times, to experiment with new programs and ideas, and to seize opportunities when they arise. Preserving financial flexibility requires sustained discipline because there are always more compelling needs than there are available resources. Trustees must have the discipline to know when to invest for the future and when to save for when a better idea comes along.

Trustees also need to ensure that the budget process produces a close alignment between the allocation of resources and the institution's mission and values. It always is tempting to spend resources on areas that are not central to the institution's mission or strategic priorities. With each budget the board should ask the question, "How does this budget advance our mission and support our core values, needs, and priorities?"

The board should understand its comfort level with investment risk. Managing the endowment and making investments entail taking risks. The investment committee needs the assurance that the whole board appreciates and approves of the degree of risk that has been taken with the management of the endowment and other capital.

To provide the right level of oversight, the board should develop with the financial management team a set of financial principles. These principles should govern the preparation of the annual budget and take a long-term perspective. In turn, an important objective of the financial principles is to achieve a state of financial equilibrium. Being in financial equilibrium requires balanced operating budgets, protected endowment purchasing power, a modernized physical plant, and adequate support to sustain faculty and staff.

Financial information should be accurate, reliable, and understandable for the board and the general public. If the board is concerned that the information it receives is inaccurate, the first order of business is to change that situation.

An appropriate way for the board to excise its financial responsibilities is to carefully monitor the implementation of strategic plans and to ask the right questions at the right time. This is an art form, but all trustees should feel comfortable asking *any* question about the financial condition of their institution. Failure to ask the question is a failure to exercise responsible trusteeship. An especially important role for trustees is to focus on the assumptions used for long-range projections.

There should be a partnership between the senior financial team and the board that nurtures trust and understanding of the roles of the board and the financial-management staff. There should be no surprises from management, and the board should appreciate the time pressures and complex issues the financial team confronts on a regular basis.

A Checklist for Exercising Financial Responsibility. The following checklist of good policies and practices can help a board assess how effectively it is fulfilling its financial responsibilities:

• Does the board have a clear understanding of the institution's current revenue and expense realities and its strategic financial issues?

• Does the board have confidence in the financial-management and board-oversight teams?

• Are there adequate controls and accounting systems in place? Are reports timely, accurate, and understandable?

• Is there a long-range plan, and is the board regularly monitoring its progress?

• Does the board practice due diligence on major financial decisions?

• Does the budget process appropriately reflect the institution's culture and traditions?

• Does the annual budget advance the institution's mission, priorities, and values?

• Has the board developed and approved a set of financial principles to guide resource-allocation decisions and long-range plans?

• Is the institution in a state of financial equilibrium?

• Does the board understand basic facts about the tuition, scholarships, and debt burdens of students?

• Is the board comfortable with the amount of risk that has been taken with the investment of the endowment?

• Does the institution carry adequate property and liability insurance, including insurance to cover the trustees?

• Does the administration have the will and the courage to practice "growth by substitution"?

• Does the administration have a plan for cost containment?

• Does the institution invest in maintaining and upgrading the professional competence and skills in its professors and administrative and support staffs?

• Is there enough financial flexibility to enable the institution to invest in new ideas and programs?

• Does the board understand where the institution stands competitively with its cohort of peers?

• Does the institution have the capacity and the will to adapt to the changing world?

• Is the board able and comfortable asking difficult questions of management (and does management accept this board responsibility)?

• Does the board have 100 percent participation in annual and capital fund-raising efforts?

Linking Strategic Planning and Fund-Raising With Financial Responsibility. Strategic planning and fund-raising are important parts of the overarching financial responsibility of boards to be prudent stewards of institutional assets. A discussion of the financial responsibilities of governing boards would not be complete without touching upon these two related activities.

Strategic planning is about using assets to advance the institution's mission and values—to help articulate a vision for the future. Fund-raising provides the financial resources to make the vision a reality. Both are integral parts of setting and maintaining institutional direction.

The level of board involvement in strategic planning depends on the institution's culture, history, and financial condition. In some institutions, senior management alone handles strategic planning and presents a plan to the board for review and approval. In others

(and much more appropriately), a broad-based committee of trustees, administrators, faculty, students, and even alumni devise the strategic plan—with or without the use of outside expertise. In setting goals and priorities, a close partnership should exist among the board, administration, and faculty. The board does not have to be responsible for developing the strategic plan, but it does have responsibility to ensure that there is a good plan resulting from a good process—and that it helps develop the plan in appropriate ways. The trustees should feel considerable ownership of the plan if they are going to be motivated to help with fund-raising strategies and implementation. A successful planning effort can energize the community, build confidence in the administration and the board, provide needed focus, be an instrument of change, and reaffirm the institution's fundamental values and mission.

A major fund-raising effort often follows the development of a strategic plan. Inevitably, new ideas and programs emerge from the strategic plan that require new sources of support and financial backing. The board has a major responsibility to assist as advocates, participants, and donors.

Trustees can be powerful and effective advocates with prospective donors, whom they can help identify. As ambassadors, they can talk to their friends and colleagues, alumni, and parents about the important work that needs to be done. They can become enthusiastic storytellers about the difference a gift will make. The positive energy from the board can provide a strong motivation for the president and the development office. The board can help create a climate for giving that is indispensable to fund-raising success.

Trustees can be active participants in fund-raising strategies. They can identify prospects, cultivate prospects, solicit gifts, and ensure that donors are properly thanked and recognized. They also can ensure that the gifts are used in accordance with the donor's intentions and that the institution is a good steward of the funds entrusted to it.

And finally, the board needs to lead by example. If trustees are going to solicit donations, they need to have good records of giving themselves. Donors often want to know whether the solicitor has personally committed to the campaign, and sometimes they want to know the size of the gift. If the board does not have 100 percent participation, the task of asking others for support is much more difficult. It is a financial responsibility of trustees to make gifts commensurate with their resources and responsibilities. With financial responsibility comes the obvious obligation for personal financial support.

Looking Ahead. No one knows what the future holds. The decade of the 1990s was good to most of higher education, but the 21st century surely will present new challenges and opportunities. The financial responsibilities of governing boards will continue to evolve, but the core responsibilities described in this book are unlikely to change. External events and changing societal needs, coupled with the sheer pace of technological change, will require boards to think more strategically and to preserve as much financial flexibility as possible. The functions and strategic importance of citizen boards will become more significant. Those institutions that survive and thrive
will be the ones that have the best combination of management and governance, leadership, commitment, vision, and resources.

Several trends already are evident that present challenges and opportunities for boards. These issues have profound financial implications.

• *Cost containment.* The concern with the cost of a college education is not new. It was a hot issue for higher education during the 1990s. But it has yet to be satisfactorily addressed as the rates of growth in tuition continue to outpace inflation. The issue of how accessible and affordable our institutions are to the general public remains troublesome. The public's tolerance for the high-cost, low-productivity paradigm that has characterized much of higher education seems to be growing thin. The pressure to expand services, courses, and support is mounting at the same time there is pressure to rein in costs. Trustees will have to confront the unpleasant topics of productivity, efficiency, and the need for new ways to deliver the educational product. Institutions that can deliver cost-effective, high-quality education will leave behind those that continue to conduct their business as usual. Trustees must push for a thoughtful and strategic process for addressing the cost issue. This will involve examining both the administrative and academic operations. Any discussion of the delivery of the academic product goes to the heart of the institution's value system and is bound to raise tensions. But costs cannot be contained without changing the current paradigms. Trustees should reject the argument that costs cannot be cut without necessarily lowering quality.

• *Competition from outside the academy.* Closely related to the cost-effective delivery of education is the growing number of for-profit firms that have entered the higher education marketplace. These firms are much more business oriented and do not pretend to offer the same experience as a residential college or a research university.

Instead, they are focused on how students learn and on assessing the effectiveness of their teaching methods. They understand the importance of scalability, of developing course content that is effective, and of delivering it in the same way in multiple courses. They seek to serve those who are eager for a college education but have neither the resources nor the time to acquire a college degree in the traditional way. They are trying to capture the growing market of life-long learners by making learning opportunities more compatible with lifestyles and career needs.

Over time, these for-profit entities conceivably could become more attractive to the traditional-aged student.

Boards would be wise to watch these developments and make certain their institution is assessing teaching methods and ways to adapt to the changing needs of learners.

• *Faculty as entrepreneurs.* There are increasing opportunities for faculty members to augment their salaries by working outside their institutions. The social contract with faculty may come under increased pressure as institutions struggle to make certain their faculties are focused on the needs of their institutions while providing opportunities for professional growth. The responsibilities and duties of the tenured faculty may have to be reexamined to ensure the primacy of their teaching and research responsibilities. For faculty members who deliver their courses over the Internet, clear policies on who owns the course along with complicated copyright issues will have to be resolved.

• *Advances in information technology.* The information-technology revolution simultaneously creates a threat and an opportunity. Powerful computers and networks can deliver educational services to anyone at any place and any time. Students no longer need be confined to the campus or constrained by the academic calendar. At the same time, the technological revolution creates an opportunity to augment the traditional lecture with powerful tools, help students learn in new ways, and conduct global classes. But this is not easy. It is difficult to keep up with the rapid changes and attract and retain the staff needed to run and service the computers and the networks. The opportunity to teach a broader group of students and to deliver education in a new way is open to all institutions. Many pedagogical and financial issues need to be addressed, of course. Any institution that feels it will not be affected by the technological revolution is in denial. The board must make certain that the best minds in their institution develop a strategy for dealing with distance education and providing technologically enhanced courses appropriate to its mission.

• *Serving a more diverse society.* Current projections indicate that almost 40 percent of all Americans will be members of minority groups by the third decade of this century. The growth in the diversity of our population means that the composition of the faculty and staff needs to change to keep pace with the new demographics. Educating such diverse populations of students will put pressure on the curriculum—for new courses related to students' cultural backgrounds, for testing of antiquated assumptions concerning academic programs, and for inevitable concerns over how to deal with social prejudices. The challenge will be for our institutions to prepare our students to be good citizens and to be comfortable and confident working in a more diverse, global world.

• *Improving competitiveness through collaboration.* Colleges and universities are inherently competitive. It is in their nature to want to improve their academic standing. They want to improve the academic quality of their students, the quality of their faculty, and their

academic reputation among peer institutions. Yet more institutions are entering into partnerships with one another to save money and improve efficiency. There is a growing recognition that the consumer does not care who provides administrative services as long as the service is good, or whether a professor teaches at another institution as long as the class is well taught. Trustees should encourage collaboration and support innovative ways of delivering administrative services and education. For many institutions, increased collaboration requires a painful cultural shift. Those colleges able to collaborate and still retain their institutional uniqueness and distinctiveness will be much better off than those that fear they will compromise their competitive advantage by sharing their resources and talents with others.

Trustees who are fortunate enough to serve their institutions in this new age will face challenges that few have faced before. Many believe that higher education is facing its most transformational period ever. This remains to be seen. What is certain is that the years ahead will not be dull. In the end, the future belongs to those who care enough to work their visions into practical, sustainable realities.

Recommended Readings

Board Basics: "The Board's Role in Fund-Raising," by Richard D. Legon. AGB, 1997.

Board Basics: "Understanding the Planning Process," by Raymond Hass. AGB, 1997.

"Beyond Strategic Planning: How To Involve Nonprofit Boards in Growth and Change," by Douglas C. Eadie. National Center for Nonprofit Boards, 1995.

The Board Member's Guide to Strategic Planning, by Fisher Howe. National Center for Nonprofit Boards, 1997.

Designs for Fund-Raising: Principles, Patterns, Techniques, by Harold J. Seymore, 2nd ed. Fund Raising Institute, 1988.

Educational Fund-Raising: Principles and Practice, by Michael Worth & Associates. Oryx Press, 1993.

Fund-Raising Leadership: A Guide for College and University Boards, by J.W. Pocock. AGB, 1989.

The Leadership Challenge, by James M. Kouzes and Barry Z. Posner. Jossey-Bass Publishers, 1995.

Restructuring Higher Education, by Terrence J. MacTaggart and Associates. Jossey-Bass Publishers, 1996.

The Rise and Fall of Strategic Planning, by Henry Mintzberg. The Free Press, 1994.

Strategic Decision Making: Key Questions and Indicators for Trustees, by Carol Frances, George Huxel, Joel W. Meyerson, and Dabney G. Park, Jr. AGB, 1989.

Strategic Planning For Colleges and Universities: A Systems Approach to Planning and Resource Allocation, by John C. Merson and Robert L. Qualls. Trinity University Press, 1979.

Strategic Planning for Public and Nonprofit Organizations, by John M. Bryson. Jossey-Bass Publishers, 1988.